TEACHER'S GUIDE

daybook, *n.* a book in which the events of the day are recorded; *specif.* a journal or diary

DAYBOOK

of Critical Reading and Writing

GRADE 6

CONSULTING AUTHORS

FRAN CLAGGETT

LOUANN REID

RUTH VINZ

Great Source Education Group
a Houghton Mifflin Company
Wilmington, Massachusetts

www.greatsource.com

C o n s u l t i n g   A u t h o r s

Fran Claggett, currently an educational consultant for schools throughout the country and teacher at Sonoma State University, taught high school English for more than thirty years. She is author of several books, including *Drawing Your Own Conclusions: Graphic Strategies for Reading, Writing, and Thinking* (1992) and *A Measure of Success* (1996).

Louann Reid taught junior and senior high school English, speech, and drama for nineteen years and currently teaches courses for future English teachers at Colorado State University. Author of numerous articles and chapters, her first books were *Learning the Landscape* and *Recasting the Text* with Fran Claggett and Ruth Vinz (1996).

Ruth Vinz, currently a professor and director of English education at Teachers College, Columbia University, taught in secondary schools for twenty-three years. She is author of several books and numerous articles that discuss teaching and learning in the English classroom as well as a frequent presenter, consultant, and co-teacher in schools throughout the country.

Printed in the United States of America

International Standard Book Number: 0-669-46445-7

6 7 8 9 10 -POO- 04 03 02 01

Great Source wishes to acknowledge the many insights and improvements made to the *Daybooks* thanks to the work of the following teachers and educators.

R e a d e r s

Jay Amberg
Glenbrook South High School
Glenview, Illinois

Joanne Arellanes
Rancho Cordova, California

Nancy Bass
Moore Middle School
Arvada, Colorado

Jim Benny
Sierra Mountain Middle School
Truckee, California

Noreen Benton
Guilderland High School
Altamont, New York

Janet Bertucci
Hawthorne Junior High School
Vernon Hills, Illinois

Jim Burke
Burlingame High School
Burlingame, California

Mary Castellano
Hawthorne Junior High School
Vernon Hills, Illinois

Diego Davalos
Chula Vista High School
Chula Vista, California

Jane Detgen
Daniel Wright Middle School
Lake Forest, Illinois

Michelle Ditzian
Sheperd Junior High School
Deerfield, Illinois

Jenni Dunlap
Highland Middle School
Libertyville, Illinois

Judy Elman
Highland Park High School
Highland Park, Illinois

Mary Ann Evans-Patrick
Fox Valley Writing Project
Oshkosh, Wisconsin

Howard Frishman
Twin Grove Junior High School
Buffalo Grove, Illinois

Kathleen Gaynor
Wheaton, Illinois

Beatrice Gerrish
Bell Middle School
Golden, Colorado

Kathy Glass
San Carlos, California

Alton Greenfield
Minnesota Dept. of Child, Family &
Learning
St. Paul, Minnesota

Sue Hebson
Deerfield High School
Deerfield, Illinois

Carol Jago
Santa Monica High School
Santa Monica, California

Diane Kepner
Oakland, California

Lynne Ludwig
Gregory Middle School
Naperville, Illinois

Joan Markos-Horejs
Fox Valley Writing Project
Oshkosh, Wisconsin

James McDermott
South High Community School
Worcester, Massachusetts

Tim McGee
Worland High School
Worland, Wyoming

Mary Jane Mulholland
Lynn Classical High School
Lynn, Massachusetts

Lisa Myers
Englewood, Colorado

Karen Neilsen
Desert Foothills Middle School
Phoenix, Arizona

Jayne Allen Nichols
El Camino High School
Sacramento, California

Mary Nicolini
Penn Harris High School
Mishawaka, Indiana

Lucretia Pannozzo
John Jay Middle School
Katonah, New York

Robert Pavlick
Marquette University
Milwaukee, Wisconsin

Linda Popp
Gregory Middle School
Naperville, Illinois

Caroline Ratliffe
Fort Bend Instructional School District
Sugar Land, Texas

Guerrino Rich
Akron North High School
Akron, Ohio

Shirley Rosson
Alief Instructional School District
Houston, Texas

Alan Ruter
Glenbrook South High School
Glenview, Illinois

Rene Schillenger
Washington, D.C.

Georgianne Schulte
Oak Park Middle School
Oak Park, Illinois

Carol Schultz
Tinley Park, Illinois

Wendell Schwartz
Adlai E. Stevenson High School
Lincolnshire, Illinois

Lynn Snell
Oak Grove School
Green Oaks, Illinois

Hildi Spritzer
Oakland, California

Bill Stone
Plano Senior High School
Plano, Texas

Barbara Thompson
Hazelwood School
Florissant, Missouri

Elma Torres
Orange Grove Instructional School
District Orange Grove, Texas

Bill Weber
Libertyville High School
Libertyville, Illinois

Darby Williams
Sacramento, California

Hillary Zunin
Napa High School
Napa, California

Table of Contents

Overview

What is a daybook and what is it good for? These are the first questions asked about this series, *Daybooks of Critical Reading and Writing.*

The answer is that a daybook is a keepable, journal-like book that helps improve students' reading and writing. *Daybooks* are a tool to promote daily reading and writing in classrooms. By immersing students in good literature and by asking them to respond creatively to it, the *Daybooks* combine critical reading and creative, personal response to literature.

The literature in each *Daybook* has been chosen to complement the selections commonly found in anthologies and the most commonly taught novels. Most of the literature selections are brief and designed to draw students into them by their brevity and high-interest appeal. In addition, each passage has a literary quality that will be probed in the lesson.

Each lesson focuses on a specific aspect of critical reading—that is, the reading skills used by good readers. These aspects of critical reading are summarized in closing statements positioned at the end of each lesson. To organize this wide-ranging analysis into critical reading, the consulting authors have constructed a framework called the "Angles of Literacy."

This framework organizes the lessons and units in the *Daybook*. The five Angles of Literacy described here are:

- marking or annotating the text
- examining the story connections
- looking at authors' perspectives
- studying the language and craft of a text
- focusing on individual authors

The Angles of Literacy are introduced in the first cluster of the *Daybook* and then explored in greater depth in subsequent clusters.

The *Daybook* concept was developed to help teachers with a number of practical concerns:

1. To introduce daily (or at least weekly) critical reading and writing into classrooms

2. To fit into the new configurations offered by block scheduling

3. To create a literature book students can own, allowing them to mark up the literature and write as they read

4. To make an affordable literature book that students can carry home

How to Use the Daybook

As the *Daybooks* were being developed, more than fifty teachers commented on and reviewed the lesson concept and individual lessons and units. Middle school teachers helped shape the choice of literature and the skills to be taught. From their efforts and our discussions, several main uses for the *Daybooks* emerged.

1. Supplementing an Anthology

For literature teachers stuck with dated anthologies, the *Daybooks* appeared to offer an easy, economical means of updating their literature curriculums. The multitude of contemporary authors and wide range of multicultural authors fit nicely with older and soon-to-become out-of-date anthology series.

2. Supplementing a List of Core Novels

For middle schools guided by a list of core readings, the *Daybooks* offered a convenient way to add some daily writing and critical reading instruction to classes. Plus, the emphasis on newer, young adult writers seemed to these teachers just right for their courses laden with "classics."

3. Adding a New Element

Some middle school teachers use the *Daybooks* to add literature to their curriculum; some use them to add an element of critical reading to what is already a literature-based approach; other teachers rely on the *Daybooks* to add the element of daily reading and writing to their curriculum. Teachers have found a number of different ways to slot the *Daybooks* into their curriculums, mostly because of their three-way combination of literature, critical reading, and daily creative writing.

4. Block Scheduling

Daybook activities were also designed to accommodate new block-scheduled class periods. With longer periods, teachers commented on the need to introduce 2-4 parts to each "block," one of which would be a *Daybook* lesson. The brief, self-contained lessons fit perfectly at the beginning or end of a block and could be used to complement or build upon another segment of the day.

The reviewers of the *Daybooks* proved that no two classrooms are alike. While each was unique in its own way, every teacher found use for the *Daybook* lessons in the classroom. In the end, the usefulness of the *Daybooks* derived from the blend of elements they alone offer:

- direct instruction of how to read critically
- regular and explicit practice in marking up and annotating texts
- "writing to learn" activities for each day or week
- great selections from contemporary (and often multicultural) literature
- in-depth instruction in how to read literature and write effectively about it

Organization of the Daybooks

Each *Daybook* has 14 units, or clusters, of five lessons. A lesson is designed to last approximately 30 minutes, although some lessons will surely extend longer depending on how energetically students attack the writing activities. But the intent throughout was to create brief, potent lessons that integrate quality literature, critical reading instruction, and writing.

The unifying concept behind these lessons is the angles of literacy—the idea that a selection can be approached from at least five directions:

• by annotating and marking up the text

• by analyzing the story connections in the literature

• by examining authors' perspectives

• by studying the language and craft of the writer

• by focusing closely on all of the aspects of a single writer's work

A lesson typically begins with an introduction and leads quickly into a literary selection. By looking closely at the selection, students are able to discover what can be learned through careful reading. Students are led to look again at the selection and to respond analytically, reflectively, and creatively to what they have read. An Answer Key at the back of this book provides selected sample responses.

boldface terms in glossary

stanza, a group of lines that are set off to form a division in POETRY.

structural clues, a vocabulary strategy in which the reader breaks down...

focus on critical reading

lesson title

initial response activity

unit title

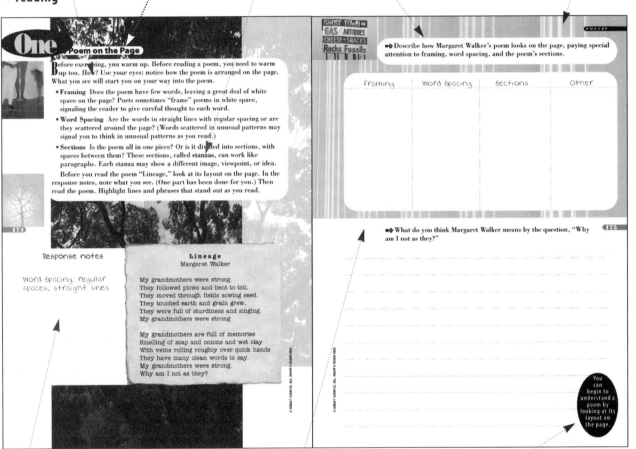

One **Poem on the Page**

Before exercising, you warm up. Before reading a poem, you need to warm up too. How? Use your eyes: notice how the poem is arranged on the page. What you see will start you on your way into the poem.

• **Framing** Does the poem have few words, leaving a great deal of white space on the page? Poets sometimes "frame" poems in white space, signaling the reader to give careful thought to each word.

• **Word Spacing** Are the words in straight lines with regular spacing or are they scattered around the page? (Words scattered in unusual patterns may signal you to think in unusual patterns as you read.)

• **Sections** Is the poem all in one piece? Or is it divided into sections, with spaces between them? These sections, called stanzas, can work like paragraphs. Each stanza may show a different image, viewpoint, or idea.

Before you read the poem "Lineage," look at its layout on the page. In the response notes, note what you see. (One part has been done for you.) Then read the poem. Highlight lines and phrases that stand out as you read.

Response notes

Word spacing: regular spaces, straight lines

Lineage
Margaret Walker

My grandmothers were strong.
They followed plows and bent to toil.
They moved through fields sowing seed.
They touched earth and grain grew.
They were full of sturdiness and singing.
My grandmothers were strong.

My grandmothers are full of memories
Smelling of soap and onions and wet clay
With veins rolling roughly over quick hands
They have many clean words to say.
My grandmothers were strong.
Why am I not as they?

➡ Describe how Margaret Walker's poem looks on the page, paying special attention to framing, word spacing, and the poem's sections.

Framing	Word Spacing	Sections	Other

➡ What do you think Margaret Walker means by the question, "Why am I not as they?"

You can begin to understand a poem by looking at its layout on the page.

space for annotations

longer, interpretive response to literature

summary statement

F r e q u e n t l y   A s k e d   Q u e s t i o n s

One benefit of the extensive field-testing of the *Daybooks* was to highlight right at the beginning several questions about the *Daybooks*.

1. What is a daybook anyway?

A daybook used to be "a book in which daily transactions are recorded" or "a diary." Most recently, the word has been used to mean "journal." To emphasize the daily reading and writing, the authors chose the word *daybook* rather than *journal*. And, indeed, the *Daybooks* are much more than journals, in that they include literature selections and instruction in critical reading.

2. Are students supposed to write in the *Daybook*?

Yes, definitely. Only by physically marking the text will students become active readers. To interact with a text and take notes as an active reader, students must write in their *Daybooks*. Students will have a written record of their thoughts, questions, brainstorms, annotations, and creative responses. The immediacy of reading and responding on the page is an integral feature of the *Daybooks*. Students will also benefit from the notebook-like aspect, allowing them to double back to earlier work, see progress, store ideas, and record responses. The *Daybook* serves, in a way, like a portfolio. It is one simple form of portfolio assessment.

3. Can I photocopy these lessons?

No, unfortunately, you cannot. The selections, instruction, and activities are protected by copyright. To copy them infringes on the rights of the authors of the selections and the book. Writers such as Langston Hughes, Cynthia Rylant, and Ray Bradbury have granted permission for the use of their work in the *Daybooks* and to photocopy their work violates their copyright.

4. Can I skip around in the *Daybook*?

Yes, absolutely. The *Daybooks* were designed to allow teachers maximum flexibility. You can start with some of the later clusters (or units) and then pick up the earlier ones later on in the year. Or you can teach a lesson from here and one from there. But the optimum order of the book is laid out in the table of contents, and students will most likely see the logic and continuity of the book when they start at the beginning and proceed in order.

5. What is "annotating a text"? Are students supposed to write in the margin of the book?

Annotating refers to underlining parts of a text, circling words or phrases, highlighting with a colored marker, or taking notes in the margin. Students begin their school years marking up books in kindergarten and end, often in college, writing in the margins of their texts or highlighting key passages. Yet in the years in between—the majority of their school years—students are often forbidden from writing in their books, even though it represents a natural kinesthetic aid for memory and learning.

6. Why were these literature selections chosen?

The literature was chosen primarily for its high interest for students. Middle school teachers advised the editors how to construct a table of contents that had the selections with proven student appeal. The first, and foremost, criterion was the appeal of a selection for students.

But the literature was also carefully matched with the lesson concept. (A lesson on characters, for example, needed to present two or three strong characters for study.) So, in addition to high student appeal, the selections illustrate a specific aspect of critical reading and are representative of the diversity of our society.

7. What are the art and photos supposed to represent?

The art program for the *Daybooks* features the work of outstanding contemporary photographers. These photos open each unit and set the tone. Then, within each lesson, a number of smaller, somewhat enigmatic images are used. The purpose behind these images is not to illustrate what is happening in the literature or even to represent an interpretation of it. Rather, the hope is to stretch students' minds, hinting at connections, provoking the imagination, jarring loose a random thought or two about the selection. And, of course, the hope is that students will respond favorably to contemporary expressions of creativity.

8. In what way do the *Daybooks* teach critical thinking skills?

One of the hallmarks of the middle school *Daybooks* is their emphasis on critical reading skills, such as predicting, inferencing, and evaluating. On the advice of practicing teachers, the middle school *Daybooks* purposely emphasized the key skills students need to improve their reading skills, such as finding the main idea, distinguishing fact from opinion, making inferences, reflecting on what you read, and so forth. In fact, critical thinking skills are taught across the grades, as the scope and sequence chart in this guide on pages 11-12 shows. The *Daybooks* are a marriage of strong teaching of critical reading skills with good literature and the consistent opportunity to write about what you read.

9. What are the boldface terms in the lesson all about?

The terms boldfaced in the lessons appear in the back of the *Daybook*. The glossary includes key literary terms that 1) are used in the *Daybook* lessons, and 2) students are likely to encounter in literature classes. The glossary is another resource for students to use in reading and reacting to the literature.

Skill Instruction	Grade 6	Grade 7	Grade 8
Comprehension			
author's perspective/viewpoint	✓	✓	✓
author's purpose	✓	✓	✓
bias	✓	✓	
cause and effect	✓	✓	✓
change pace	✓		✓
compare and contrast	✓	✓	✓
details	✓	✓	✓
draw conclusions		✓	✓
evaluate	✓	✓	✓
fact and opinion	✓	✓	✓
generalize			✓
inference	✓	✓	✓
make connections to personal life	✓	✓	✓
predict	✓	✓	✓
reflect	✓	✓	✓
respond to literature	✓	✓	✓
sequence	✓		
summarize	✓		✓
thesis statement	✓		✓
visualize		✓	✓
Literary Elements/Author's Craft			
alliteration	✓		✓
author's style	✓	✓	✓
characterization	✓	✓	✓
imagery	✓	✓	
irony	✓	✓	✓
metaphor	✓	✓	✓
mood	✓	✓	
onomatopoeia		✓	
personification	✓	✓	✓
plot	✓	✓	✓
point of view	✓	✓	✓
repetition, rhyme, rhythm	✓	✓	✓
sensory language	✓	✓	✓
setting	✓	✓	✓
simile	✓	✓	✓
symbolism		✓	
text structure	✓	✓	✓
theme	✓	✓	✓
tone	✓	✓	✓
word choice	✓	✓	✓

Skill Instruction	Grade 6	Grade 7	Grade 8
Study and Word Skills			
formulate questions	✓	✓	
highlight	✓	✓	✓
preview	✓		✓
take notes	✓	✓	✓
use context clues	✓		
use graphic sources	✓	✓	✓
use structural clues	✓	✓	✓

Correlation to Write Source 2000

Like the *Write Source 2000* handbook, the *Daybooks* will appeal to certain teachers who need versatile, flexible materials and who place a premium on books with high student appeal. Some teachers, by nature, are more eclectic in their teaching approach, and others are more consistent and patterned. Some teachers place a premium on student interest and relevance more than on structured, predictable lessons. The *Daybooks*, like *Write Source 2000*, are directed at more eclectic teachers and classrooms.

The *Daybooks* are organized to allow maximum flexibility. You can pick an individual lesson or cluster of lessons in order to feature a certain author or literary selection. Or, you may want to concentrate on a particular area of critical reading. In either case, the *Daybooks*, like *Write Source 2000,* allow you to pick up the book and use it for days or weeks at a time, then leave it, perhaps to teach a novel or longer writing project, and then return to it again later in the semester. You, not the text, set the classroom agenda.

Another similarity between the *Daybooks* and the *Write Source 2000* handbook lies in the approach to writing. Both begin from the premise that writing is, first and foremost, a means of discovery. "Writing to learn" is the common expression for this idea. Only by expression can we discover what lies within us. *Write Source 2000* introduces this idea in its opening chapter, and the *Daybooks*, by promoting daily writing, give you the tool to make writing a consistent, regular feature of your classes.

But the *Daybooks* only start students on a daily course of reading and writing. Individual writing assignments are initiated but not carried through to final drafts. The purpose of writing in the *Daybooks* is mostly one of discovery, creative expression, clarification of ideas or interpretations, and idea generation. The *Daybooks* are intended to be starting points, places to ruminate and organize thoughts about literature, as opposed to offering definitive instructions about how to craft an essay or write a persuasive letter. That's where *Write Source 2000* comes in. It picks up where the *Daybooks* leave off, providing everything students need to create a polished essay or literary work.

The accompanying chart correlates writing assignments in the *Daybooks* to *Write Source 2000.*

Daybook Lesson	Writing Activity	*Write Source 2000* reference
Angles of Literacy		
1. Becoming an Active Reader	react to a story	175-181, 345
2 . Connecting with the Story	write a journal entry	48, 145-148
3. Language and Craft	write note cards	225-226, 352
4. An Author's Perspective	complete a chart	304-305
5. Focus on the Writer	introduce an author	63, 123

Daybook Lesson	Writing Activity	*Write Source 2000* reference
Essentials of Reading		
1. Thinking with the Writer	continue a story	184-191
2. Reading Between the Lines	write a journal entry	48, 145-148
3. Managing the Main Idea	write about an experience	126, 153-159
4. Author's Purpose	evaluate types of writing	342
5. Reflecting on Reading	respond to a poem	180, 196-197
Essentials of Story		
1. A Story's Setting	create a scene	188-189
2. A Story's Characters	make a word picture	136, 188, 343
3. A Story's Point of View	rewrite a scene	190, 344
4. A Story's Plot	summarize a plot	214-216
5. A Story's Theme	describe an experience	126, 153-159
Understanding Character		
1. A Character's Appearance	create a character	188
2. A Character's Actions	write a speech	350-351
3. A Character's Speech	analyze a character	287
4. A Character's Thought and Feelings	write a journal entry	48, 145-148
5. The Other Characters	write a scene	188-190
Author's Craft		
1. Surprising Comparisons	create similes	140
2. What It Is	make a Venn diagram	56, 313
3. Almost Human	personify an object	140
4. See It, Hear It, Feel It...	continue a poem	198-200
5. It's a Twist	explain a poem	196, 202-207
The Art of Argument		
1. What's It All About?	write a letter to the editor	121-122, 242-250, 292-293
2. With Good Reason	construct an argument	121-122, 292-296
3. Seeing the Other Side	write a paragraph	98-99, 104-106
4. That's a Fact!	list facts	292
5. Good Point?	write a persuasive proposal	121-122, 289, 291-296

Daybook Lesson	Writing Activity	*Write Source 2000* reference
Active Reading: Poetry		
1. The Poem on the Page	explore a poem	196-197
2. Tuning In	make a sketch	196-197
3. Beyond Words	write a poem	198-207
4. Word Music	continue a poem	198-200
5. The Beat Goes On	evaluate poems	196-197, 289
Active Reading: Persuasive Writing		
1. The Emotional Impact of Words	vary connotations	136
2. Where Is the Writer Coming From?	write to an author	150-152, 181
3. Taking Sides	explore bias	289-290, 298
4. Separating Fact from Opinion	write notes	225, 292-293, 321
5. Tone	examine tone	143, 344-345
Focus on the Writer: Gary Paulsen		
1. An Author's Style	continue a story	184-185, 188-192
2. Real-Life Characters	plan a character sketch	188
3. Personal Challenges	describe a character	188
4. Challenges in Nature	complete a character chart	188,
5. Autobiographical Writing	describe an experience	126, 153-159

Angles of Literacy

by Louann Reid

When we view something of potential value, such as a diamond or an antique vase, we often examine it from all sides. We hold it up and slowly turn it, looking first at the front, then the sides and back. Combining information from each perspective, we construct a fuller picture of the object and its worth.

Similarly, we can examine a concept or idea from several angles, or perspectives, using a variety of approaches to understand a complex concept. Perhaps no concept in education is more complex—or more important—than literacy.

"Literacy" is frequently defined as the ability to read and write. But people also need to be able to read critically, write effectively, draw diagrams, collaborate with others, listen carefully, and understand complex instructions. In short, literacy means being able to do whatever is required to communicate effectively in a variety of situations. Angles of Literacy is the term we use in these *Daybooks* to identify five approaches to becoming literate.

THE FIVE ANGLES

The Angles of Literacy are major perspectives from which to examine a text. Strategies within each angle further define each one. Activities in the *Daybooks* provide students with multiple opportunities to become autonomous users of the strategies on other literature that they will encounter.

The angles are listed in an order that reflects the way that readers and writers first engage with the text. They are encouraged to move gradually from that initial engagement to a more evaluative or critical stance where they study the author's language and craft, life, and work. They critique the texts they read and consider what other critics have written. Moving from engagement through interpretation to evaluation is the process that Louise Rosenblatt and later reader-response critics advocate.

In our own work with middle school and secondary school students, we have repeatedly seen the value of encouraging students to read and write using all three stages—engagement, interpretation, evaluation. We also know that students sometimes begin at a different stage in the process—perhaps with interpretation rather than engagement. So, our five angles are not meant to be a hierarchy. Students may begin their engagement with the text using any angle and proceed in any order. Depending on the text and the context, readers might start with making personal connections to the stories in an essay. If the text is by an author that the students know well, they might naturally begin by comparing this work to the author's other works.

STRATEGIES

Strategies are plans or approaches to learning. By using some strategies over and over, students can learn to comprehend any text. The *Daybook* activities, such as annotating or visualizing a specific poem, story, or essay, provide students multiple opportunities to develop these strategies. From using this scaffolding students gradually become more independent readers and, ultimately, fully literate.

Because strategies are employed through activities, it may seem at first that they are the same thing. Yet, it is important to remember that a strategy is a purposeful plan. When, as readers, we select a strategy such as underlining key phrases, we have selected this action deliberately to help us differentiate between important information and unimportant information. We may use a double-entry log (an activity) to identify the metaphors in a poem. Our purpose in doing so is to understand figurative language (a strategy).

At the end of each lesson, the strategies are explicitly stated. In a sentence or two, the main point of the activity is noted. When students complete all 70 lessons in a daybook, they will have 70 statements of what they, as active readers, can do to read critically and write effectively.

Reflection is a vital component in helping students understand the use of strategies. After using a particular strategy, students need to step back and consider whether the strategy worked or did not work. They might think about how an approach or a strategy can change their understanding of what they read and write. Students might ask themselves a series of questions such as: What have I done? What have I learned? What would I do differently next time? How did the angle or strategy affect my understanding? What would I understand differently if I had changed the angle or the strategy?

ACTIVITIES

Each lesson in these *Daybooks* contains activities for students. From rereading to discussing with a partner to making a story chart, students learn how to become more critical readers and more effective writers. Many activities encourage students to write to learn. Other activities encourage students to increase their understanding of a text by visualizing it in a sketch or a graphic organizer. But, as much as possible, the *Daybooks* try to encourage students to make a creative written response with a poem, some dialogue, a character sketch, or some other creative assignment.

We have selected activities that work particularly well with the texts in the lesson and with the strategies we want students to develop. However, as you will see when you and your students use the *Daybooks*, there are several possible activities that could reinforce a particular strategy. You may want to have students try some of these activities, such as making a story chart or using a double-entry log, when they read other texts in class. This would also be another opportunity to have students ask themselves the reflective questions.

A n g l e s   o f   L i t e r a c y

ANGLE OF VISION	STRATEGIES	SELECTED ACTIVITIES
Interacting with a Text	• underlining key phrases • writing questions or comments in the margin • noting word patterns and repetitions • circling unknown words • keeping track of the story or idea as it unfolds	• Write down initial impressions. • Re-read. • Write a summary of the poem. • Generate two questions and one "certainty." Then, discuss the questions and statement in a small group.
Making Connections to the Stories within a Text	• paying attention to the stories being told • connecting the stories to one's own experience • speculating on the meaning or significance of incidents	• Make a story chart with three columns—incident in the poem, significance of the incident, related incident in my life. • Write a news story of events behind the story in the poem.

Shifting Perspectives	• examining the author's viewpoint
	• analyzing arguments
	• evaluating persuasive techniques
	• forming interpretations
	• comparing texts
		• Discuss with a partner or small group how you might read a poem differently if:
		  the speaker were female
		  you believe the speaker is a parent
		• Rewrite the text from a different point of view.

Studying the Language and Craft of a Text	• understanding figurative language • looking at the way the author uses words • modeling the style of other writers • studying various kinds of literature	• Use a double-entry log to identify metaphors and the qualities implied by the comparison. • Examine the title of the poem and its relationship to the text.
Focusing on the Writer's Life and Work	• reading what the author says about the writing • reading what others say • making inferences about the connections between an author's life and work • analyzing the writer's style • paying attention to repeated themes and topics in the work by one author	• Read about the poet's life. Then make an inference chart to record evidence from the poet's life, an inference, a comparison to the poem. • Write an evaluation of the poem. Then read what one or more critics have said about the poem or poet. Finally, write a short response, either agreeing or disagreeing with the critic. Support your ideas with textual evidence.

19

Responding to Literature Through Writing

by Ruth Vinz

We have found that students' encounters with literature are enriched when they write their way toward understanding. The writing activities in the *Daybooks* are intended to help students explore and organize their ideas and reactions during and after reading. We make use of the exploratory and clarifying roles of writing through various activities.

Exploratory assignments include those through which students question, analyze, annotate, connect, compare, personalize, emulate, map, or chart aspects in the literary selections. Generally these assignments aid students' developing interpretations and reactions to the subjects, themes, or literary devices in the literature they are reading. Other writing activities offer students the opportunity to clarify their understanding of what they've read. These assignments lead students to look at other perspectives, determine the significance of what they read, and prioritize, interpret, question, and reflect on initial impressions. Further, students are asked to create literature of their own as a way of applying the concepts they're learning. Writing to clarify also involves students in reflection, where they are asked to think about their reactions and working hypotheses. Taken together, the writing activities represent a series of strategies that students can apply to the complex task of reading literature.

The writing activities included in the *Daybooks* start students on the path toward understanding. We did not take it as the function of the writing activities in this book to lead students through the writing process toward final, finished drafts. Although examples of extensions are included here in the Teacher's Guide, the writing in the *Daybooks* introduces first draft assignments that may lead into more formal writing if you, as the teacher, so choose.

You will have your own ideas about assisting students with the writing activities or extending the writing beyond the *Daybooks*. We think it's important for you to remind students that the writing in which they engage is useful for their reading outside the *Daybooks*. For example, students may use various types of maps, charts, or diagrams introduced in the *Daybooks* when they read a novel. They may find that the response notes become a strategy they use regularly. Once exposed to imitation and modeling, students may find these useful tools for understanding an author's style, language or structure. If your students develop a conscious awareness of the strategies behind the particular writing activities, they can apply these in other reading situations.

Writing assignments to explore and to clarify students' developing interpretations are incorporated in two types of activities, both of which are elaborated on below.

WRITING ABOUT LITERATURE

You will find activities in every cluster of lessons that call upon students to write about the literature they are reading. We developed these writing assignments to help facilitate, stimulate, support, and shape students' encounters with literature. We think the assignments have four purposes:

(1) to connect the literature to the students' personal experiences; (2) to re-examine the text for various purposes (language and craft, connections with other texts, shifting perspectives, developing interpretations); (3) to develop hypotheses, judgments, and critical interpretations; (4) to apply the idea behind the lesson to a new literary text or situation.

The types of writing we have used to fulfill these purposes are:

1. Response Notes

Students keep track of their initial responses to the literature by questioning, annotating, and marking up the text in various ways. The response notes are used to get students in the habit of recording what they are thinking while reading. Many times we circle back and ask them to build on what they have written with a particular focus or way of responding. In the response notes, students are encouraged to make personal connections, re-examine text, jot down ideas for their own writing, and monitor their changing responses.

2. Personal Narrative

Students write personal stories that connect or relate to what they have read. In some cases, the narratives tell the stories of students' prior reading experiences or how a literary selection relates to their life experiences. Other activities use personal narrative to apply and refine students' understanding of narrative principles.

3. Idea Fund

Students collect ideas for writing—catalogs, lists, charts, clusters, diagrams, double-entry logs, sketches, or maps. These forms of idea gathering are useful for analyzing particular literary selections and will aid the initial preparation for longer pieces of critical analysis.

4. Short Response

Students write summaries; paraphrase main themes or ideas; and compose paragraphs of description, exposition, explanation, evaluation, and interpretation.

5. Analysis

Students write short analyses that take them beyond summarizing the literary selection or their personal reactions to it. The analytic activities engage students in recognizing symbols and figures of speech and the links between events, characters, or images. Again, these short analytical responses are intended to prepare students for longer, critical interpretation that you, as a teacher, might assign.

6. Speculation

Students' speculations are encouraged by writing activities that engage them in predicting, inferring, and imagining. "What if . . .," "How might . . .," and "Imagine that . . ." are all ways in which students are invited to see further possibilities in the literature they read.

Students use writing to record and reflect on their reactions and interpretations. At times, students are asked to share their writing with others. Such sharing is another form of reflection through which students have an opportunity to "see again" their own work in the context of what others have produced.

The writing activities in the *Daybooks* will help students connect what they read with what they experience and with what they write, and also to make connections between the literary selections and literary techniques. The activities encourage students to experiment with a range of forms, choose a range of focuses, and reflect on what they have learned from these. We hope the writing serves to give students access to a kind of literary experience they can value and apply in their future reading.

WRITING LITERATURE

Within a literary work, readers find a writer's vision, but readers also co-create the vision along with the writer and learn from his or her craft. We've asked our students to write literature of their own as a way of responding to what they read. Through writing literature, students can explore facets of the original work or use the techniques of a variety of authors. Here are a number of the activities introduced in the *Daybooks*:

1. Take the Role of Writer

Students write imaginative reconstructions of gaps in a text by adding another episode, adding dialogue, rewriting the ending, adding a section before or after the original text, adding characters, or changing the setting. Such imaginative entries into the text require that students apply their knowledge of the original.

2. Imitation and Modeling

The idea of modeling and imitation is not new. Writers learn from other writers. The modeling activities are intended to help students "read like a writer." In these activities, students experiment with nuances of expression, syntactic and other structural principles, and apply their knowledge of literary devices (for example, *rhythm, imagery, metaphor*). One goal in educating students with literature is to make explicit what writers do. One way to achieve the goal is to provide models that illustrate various principles of construction.

3. Original Pieces

Students write poems, character sketches, monologues, dialogues, episodes, vignettes, and descriptions as a way to apply the knowledge about language and craft they are gaining through their reading.

4. Living Others' Perspectives

Writing from others' viewpoints encourages students to step beyond self to imagine other perspectives. Students write from a character's point of view, compose diary entries or letters, explain others' positions or opinions, and other reactions to a situation. These writing activities encourage students to explore the concerns of others and to project other perspectives through their writing.

The writing becomes a record of students' developing and changing ideas about literature. By the time students have finished all of the writing in this book, they will have used writing strategies that can assist them in all future reading.

Reading, Writing, and Assessment

by Fran Claggett

As teachers, we all cope with the complexities of assessing student performance. We must be careful readers of student work, attentive observers of student participation in various activities, and focused writers in responding to student work. We must understand the value of rewarding what students do well and encouraging them to improve. Above all, we need to make the criteria for assessment clear to students.

THE DAYBOOKS

The *Daybooks* provide visible accounts of many aspects of the reading process. Students record all the various permutations of active reading and writing. In the current view of most teachers and researchers, reading is a process of constructing meaning through transactions with a text. In this view, the individual reader assumes responsibility for interpreting a text guided not only by the language of the text but also by the associations, cultural experiences, and prior knowledge that the reader brings to the interpretive task. Meaning does not reside solely within the words on the page. Our view of reading emphasizes the role of the reader. Construction of meaning, rather than the gaining and displaying of knowledge, should be the goal of reading instruction. This rule is reflected throughout the *Daybooks*, which guide students in how to read, respond to, interpret, and reflect on carefully selected works of literature.

Within these lessons, students interact with a text from five angles of literacy. The *Daybooks* make it possible for both students and teachers to track students' increasing sophistication in using the angles to make sense of their reading. Through the strategies presented in the lessons, students learn to express their understanding of a text. They will do such things as show their understanding of figurative language and the importance of form; write about how characters are developed and change; and demonstrate their understanding of how a piece of literature develops.

THE ROLE OF THE TEACHER

The teacher is critical to the *Daybook* agenda. Conceivably, a teacher could pass out the *Daybooks* and turn the students loose, but that would not result in the carefully guided reading and writing that is intended. Rather, the teachers are central to student success. Because of the format of the *Daybooks*, lessons are short, each taking no more than a normal class period. They are intended to be complete in themselves, yet most teachers will see that there are numerous opportunities for extensions, elaborations, further readings, group work, and writing. The Teacher's Guide provides some suggestions; you will think of many others. The *Daybooks* offer guidelines for reading and thinking, for writing and drawing used in the service of reading. They also provide many opportunities for students to write pieces of their own, modeling, responding, interpreting, and reflecting on the pieces that they have read. Many of these pieces might lead to later revision, refining, group response, and editing. It is the teacher, however, who knows the students well enough to see which pieces would be worthwhile to work with and which it is best to leave as exercises rather than completed works.

In assessing the *Daybooks*, it is important to remember to look at the students' growing facility with the processes of reading. As is true with all learning, there will be false starts, abandoned practices, and frustrations, yet also illuminations, progress, and occasional epiphanies. No music teacher ever graded every attempt at mastering a piece of music. We, too, must resist the urge—honed by years of assessing only products or finished papers—of overassessing the *Daybooks*. We must consider them the place where students are free to think things through, change their minds, even start over. But you can be alert to what the student is doing well, what is frustrating, what needs more time. To that end, we have provided a chart which may be useful in getting a sense of how students are progressing in using angles of literacy. By duplicating the chart for each student, you can track progress through the lessons. We would like to encourage the idea of jotting down notations as you work with students during the class period or look over the *Daybooks* after class. In this way, you can amass a sizable amount of information over a grading period. Coupled with a student self-assessment, you will have tangible evidence of achievement in the *Daybooks*.

INDIVIDUAL STUDENT EIGHT-WEEK ASSESSMENT CHART

The columns for each week's lessons can be used in different ways. We suggest the number system: a 5 for insightful, imaginative thinking or responding, a 1 for a minimal attempt. Some teachers prefer the check, check-plus, check-minus system. There is even room, if you turn the chart sideways, to make some notations.

Angles of Literacy

INTERACTING WITH A TEXT	I	II	III	IV	V	VI	VII	VIII
The student demonstrates understanding by using interactive strategies such as:								
underlining key phrases								
writing questions or comments in the margin								
noting word patterns and repetitions								
circling unknown words								
keeping track of ideas as they unfold								

MAKING CONNECTIONS	I	II	III	IV	V	VI	VII	VIII
The student makes connections to the stories within a text by:								
paying attention to the stories in the text								
connecting ideas and themes in the text to personal ideas, experience, feelings, and knowledge								
making connections to other texts, movies, television shows, or other media								

SHIFTING PERSPECTIVES	I	II	III	IV	V	VI	VII	VIII
The student is able to shift perspectives to examine a text from many angles. When prompted, the student will engage in such strategies as these:								
examining the author's viewpoint								
analyzing arguments								
evaluating persuasive techniques								
comparing texts								

STUDYING THE LANGUAGE AND CRAFT OF A TEXT	I	II	III	IV	V	VI	VII	VIII
The student will demonstrate an understanding of the way language and craft operate in a text. Specifically, the student will:								
show how imagery, metaphor, and figurative language are central to literature								
demonstrate an understanding of how an author's vocabulary and use of language are integral to the overall work								
use modeling to demonstrate an understanding of style and form								
demonstrate understanding of various genres and forms of literature								

FOCUSING ON THE WRITER	I	II	III	IV	V	VI	VII	VIII
The student will demonstrate a rich understanding of a single writer's work, including:								
interpreting short texts by the author								
making inferences about the connections between an author's life and work								
analyzing the writer's style								
drawing conclusions about repeated themes and topics in an author's work								
evaluating a text or comparing works by the same author								

Unit Overview

In "Angles of Literacy," students explore the many different ways they can be active—rather than passive—readers. Active readers highlight, underline, and make notes on the text; they connect their own experiences to what they read; they pay attention to the author's language and style; they try to determine what the author's perspective is; and they understand that an author's writing grows out of his or her personal experiences. To help them focus on the techniques of active reading, students will read and respond to several different works by award-winning author Mildred Taylor.

Literature Focus

	Lesson	Literature
1.	Becoming an Active Reader	**Mildred D. Taylor,** from *Roll of Thunder, Hear My Cry* (Fiction)
2.	Connecting with the Story	**Mildred D. Taylor,** from *The Gold Cadillac* (Fiction)
3.	Language and Craft	
4.	An Author's Perspective	**Mildred D. Taylor,** from *The Friendship* (Fiction)
5.	Focus on the Writer	**Mildred D. Taylor,** from an interview (Nonfiction)

Reading Focus

1. Make a selection "your own" by jotting notes in the margin, highlighting words and phrases that seem important, and underlining words or ideas you don't understand.
2. Comparing your own experiences to those in the story is one way to become involved with the selection.
3. Active readers pay attention to the words authors use and the way they use them.
4. Recognizing author's perspective helps you understand why an author includes certain details and events.
5. Knowing about an author's life can help you better understand his or her writing.

Writing Focus

1. Do a quickwrite about your reaction to Taylor's writing.
2. Write a journal entry describing your connections to Taylor's story.
3. Make notes for a presentation about Taylor's craft.
4. Complete a chart that examines and compares Taylor's perspective in several different works.
5. Write an introduction to Taylor's life and work.

One Becoming an Active Reader

Critical Reading

FOCUS

Active readers ask questions, make predictions, jot down notes, and highlight the text as they read.

BACKGROUND

Lesson One introduces students to the idea of "active reading." To start out, students will learn how to make a selection their own by annotating each page. Encourage students to mark everything they find interesting, important, or puzzling. Whenever they have a question or comment, they should make a note in the margin.

➤ To help them "see" what active reading is all about, students will examine the annotations one student made while reading Mildred Taylor's "Author's Note" from *Roll of Thunder, Hear My Cry*.

➤ In "Author's Note," Taylor explains that her father, an accomplished storyteller, deserves the credit for Taylor's success as a writer. Taylor describes her father as steadfast and principled, but full of laughter and life as well.

➤ After they've read Taylor's "Author's Note," students will read a short excerpt from *Roll of Thunder, Hear My Cry*. This selection gives students a sense of "Mildred Taylor, the novelist" as opposed to "Mildred Taylor, the loving daughter." What students should notice is that throughout the excerpt, Taylor creates a balance between steadfastness and liveliness in much the same way her father did in real life.

FOR DISCUSSION AND REFLECTION

➤ How can marking a text help you make the selection "your own"? (When marking a text, readers' own ideas, responses, and questions become an important part of the reading process.)

➤ What questions do you have about the excerpt? (Responses will vary.)

Writing

QUICK ASSESS

Do students' quickwrites:

✓ explain their reactions to Taylor's writing?

✓ refer to particular passages?

Students will do a one-minute quickwrite explaining how they feel about Mildred Taylor's writing. As a prewriting activity, students should discuss *Roll of Thunder, Hear My Cry* in small groups.

READING AND WRITING EXTENSIONS

➤ Have students write an "author's note" to be published as a foreword to their first novel. Like Taylor does in her "Author's Note," they should focus on who has influenced their writing and why.

➤ Invite students to read all of *Roll of Thunder, Hear My Cry*. When they've finished, ask students to consider which of the characters in the book seem most similar to Taylor and her father. Have them write a short essay in which they explain the similarities.

Two Connecting with the Story

C r i t i c a l   R e a d i n g

FOCUS
Relating incidents, ideas, or characters from a story to your own life can help you become actively involved in the text.

BACKGROUND

Connecting to a story is another important part of active reading. Active readers get involved with a story by comparing elements such as character, plot, and theme to their own lives. In Lesson Two, students are asked to make a connection between *The Gold Cadillac* and their own lives.

➤ In *The Gold Cadillac* (much of which is autobiographical), Taylor tells of an African American family's journey south in a recently-purchased gold Cadillac. The farther south the family travels, the more trouble white Southerners give them about their car. To the Southerners' way of thinking, no African American family has the right to own such a beautiful car.

➤ Students should be encouraged to notice the tone of Taylor's writing. Although the excerpt hints at disturbing issues, she maintains a calm, even tone that matches the tone 'lois's father uses when reassuring his girls. Instead of preaching anger, Taylor allows the reader to become angry on his or her own. This makes for a highly involving narrative.

FOR DISCUSSION AND REFLECTION

➤ How do students "connect" to the texts they read? (Responses will vary but should focus on how an event or detail in a story reminds them of something in their own lives.)

➤ What kinds of writing do you find it easy to connect with? Why? (Answers will vary.)

➤ What kinds of writing do you find it difficult to connect with? Why? (Answers will vary.)

W r i t i n g

QUICK ASSESS
Do students' journal entries:

✓ describe their connection to the text?

✓ explore how their experience is similar (and dissimilar) to the one described in *The Gold Cadillac?*

Students are asked to write a journal entry describing one of their connections to *The Gold Cadillac*. As a prewriting activity, they will list the different ways they connected to the text.

READING AND WRITING EXTENSIONS

➤ As an additional challenge, have students choose another connection from their list and then describe that connection in a short personal narrative. Remind them to use first-person narration and to offer as many details as they can so that their readers stay interested.

➤ Ask students to choose a story or poem that they thought was either very easy or extremely difficult to connect to. Have them write a paragraph explaining why they were or were not able to connect the selection to their own lives.

Three Language and Craft

Critical Reading

FOCUS

Active readers pay attention to a writer's word choice.

BACKGROUND

In "Language and Craft," students are asked to think about words and the different ways an author can string those words together to form sentences. What's important for students to note, however, is that writing is more than just a string of sentences. Writing is a craft. It is an art in the same way that painting is an art. Some writers are known for their ability to paint word pictures with their writing. Many of Mildred Taylor's novels have such a strong narrative presence that you can still "hear" the narrator's voice long after you've finished the stories.

➤ Many of Mildred Taylor's stories are told from the point of view of Cassie, who does her best to act as an unbiased reporter of events. *The Gold Cadillac* is written in this style also, but with 'lois as the first-person narrator.

➤ In keeping with the unbiased feel of the narration, Taylor's writing style tends to be spare. Her dialogue is realistic, and the narrator's voice is natural, clear, and straightforward. Although Taylor's descriptions of setting are always thorough and vivid, her language is never flowery.

FOR DISCUSSION AND REFLECTION

➤ What are some of the elements of an author's craft? (style, structure, language)

➤ Who are some writers you can think of with distinctive styles? (Answers will vary. Students should support their responses with examples.)

➤ What did you like or dislike about Mildred Taylor's style? (Responses will vary.)

➤ Why didn't the mother like the Cadillac? (Answers will vary.)

Writing

QUICK ASSESS

Do students' notes:

✔ discuss aspects of Taylor's language and craft?

✔ support the main idea with details from Taylor's writing?

✔ draw a conclusion about Taylor's craft?

After they complete a chart about her style, students are asked to make notes for a presentation on Mildred Taylor and her craft.

READING AND WRITING EXTENSIONS

➤ Ask students to make a plot map (or flow chart) that explores what they think happens after 'lois and her family begin their journey south. Each event in the plot should be given a new line on the chart. Later, they might choose one event on their plot map to write about in some detail.

➤ Ask students to think about a favorite author, poet, or essayist. What makes the writer's style memorable? Have students explore the author's style in a chart similar to the one on page 18.

Four An Author's Perspective

Critical Reading

FOCUS

Active readers try to recognize an author's perspective.

BACKGROUND

An author's perspective can affect everything about the author's writing—his or her style, subject matter, themes, and so on. The author's background often plays a major role in shaping his or her perspective. One of the reasons Mildred Taylor is an interesting author is because she brings so many different perspectives to her work.

➤ Taylor tells her readers that she wants to show "a different kind of Black world from the one so often seen." In fact, Taylor wants to show an African American world that is very much like her own, with strong, determined, and loving family members who respect each other and work together as a group. All of her stories revolve around this solid family unit.

➤ Taylor also wants to show "the Black person as heroic." Taylor creates strong, memorable characters, all of whom are called on at one time or another to show their mettle. Taylor's fictional children, parents, and grandparents alike face poverty, bigotry, and death with calm courage and an unwavering faith in the goodness of humankind. In *The Friendship*, this courage in the face of adversity is exemplified in the character of Tom Bee.

FOR DISCUSSION AND REFLECTION

➤ What are some of the elements that shape an author's perspective? (The author's experiences, education, and emotions all play a role in shaping perspective.)

➤ Why is it important for readers to understand the author's perspective? (If you understand where an author is "coming from," you may find it easier to understand the author's meaning or viewpoint.)

➤ How would you describe Mildred Taylor's perspective? (Answers will vary. Have students review the Taylor interview if they have difficulty deciding on her perspective.)

Writing

QUICK ASSESS

Do students' charts:

✔ show an understanding of the idea of "author's perspective"?

✔ effectively compare and contrast the different Taylor selections?

Students are asked to complete a chart that explores Taylor's perspective in *The Friendship*, *The Gold Cadillac*, *Roll of Thunder, Hear My Cry*, and "Author's Note."

READING AND WRITING EXTENSIONS

➤ Have each student make a list of four or more events in their lives that have helped shape who they are. When they've finished, invite volunteers to discuss the events they have listed.

➤ Have students imagine that they observed the argument between John and Mr. Tom Bee. Then ask them to write a news story about the shooting for a local newspaper. Remind them that reporters strive to remain impartial when they write.

Five Focus on the Writer

Critical Reading

FOCUS

Mildred Taylor on listening to her family's stories:

"I began to imagine myself as a storyteller, making people laugh at their own human foibles or nod their heads with pride about some stunning feat of heroism."

BACKGROUND

Sometimes discovering information about an author's background can give readers valuable insight into the author's writing. If a reader knows, for example, that an author was raised in a home that was mostly silent, the reader can better understand why the author's stories are "noisy" with characters and conversation.

➤ In this lesson, students are asked to read "My Stories," an excerpt from an on-line interview with Mildred Taylor. In the interview, Taylor explains how her family's love of storytelling taught her the value of a good story. Even as a child, Taylor knew that she wanted to be a writer when she grew up.

➤ In the interview, Taylor offers readers some clues about many of the themes and topics she enjoys exploring in her writing. In particular, Taylor discusses the importance of family and family history; she touches on day-to-day heroism and profound acts of courage; and she explores her ideas about discrimination, saying in no uncertain terms that ours is a "society designed for" the destruction of African Americans. Students should recognize that these three themes are present in *Roll of Thunder, Hear My Cry*, *The Gold Cadillac*, and *The Friendship*.

FOR DISCUSSION AND REFLECTION

➤ Does Taylor write what she knows? Explain. (Yes. Many incidents in her stories are similar to incidents from her childhood.)

➤ Why is it no surprise that Taylor decided to be a writer? (She was taught to love stories at a young age.)

➤ How does understanding Taylor's background affect your attitude toward her writing? (Responses will vary. If students need help, review particulars of Taylor's background.)

Writing

QUICK ASSESS

Do students' introductions:

✓ reflect both Taylor's life and Taylor's fiction?

✓ include information from their charts?

Before students write an introduction to Mildred Taylor, have them work in groups to search Taylor's writing for autobiographical elements.

READING AND WRITING EXTENSIONS

➤ Encourage students to write about stories they remember from their childhood—stories their family members told or stories they read in books.

➤ Ask students to choose one Mildred Taylor novel to read. When they've finished, have them give an oral report in which they summarize the plot and discuss the parts of the story in which they can see the "real" Mildred Taylor.

Unit   Overview

In "Essentials of Reading," students will explore some of the techniques critical readers use to come to a deeper, more sophisticated understanding of a piece of writing. Students will develop and practice five skills associated with critical reading: making predictions, inferencing, finding the main idea, understanding the author's purpose, and reflecting on what the author has said.

Literature   Focus

	Lesson	Literature
1.	Thinking with the Writer	**Ray Bradbury**, "All Summer in a Day" (Short Story)
2.	Reading Between the Lines	**Ray Bradbury**, "All Summer in a Day" (Short Story)
3.	Managing the Main Idea	**Mickey Roberts**, "It's All in How You Say It" (Nonfiction)
4.	Author's Purpose	**Felice Holman,** "Holiday Dinner" (Poetry)
5.	Reflecting on Reading	

Reading   Focus

1. Making predictions about the plot helps you read actively.
2. Making inferences about the characters can help deepen your understanding of a story.
3. Recognizing the main idea helps you understand what the author has to say about a subject.
4. The author's purpose helps him or her decide what kind of a piece to write.
5. Reflection gives you a better understanding of a selection and your own responses to it.

Writing   Focus

1. Continue a story based on a prediction about what might happen next.
2. Write a journal entry as if you were a character.
3. Write a personal narrative.
4. Discuss how an author's purpose could be expressed in different genres.
5. Reflect on your connections to a poem.

One Thinking with the Writer

Critical Reading

FOCUS

Active readers make predictions about what will happen next.

BACKGROUND

The first reading essential students will consider is making predictions. As students may already know, making predictions while reading is a "win-win" proposition for writers and readers alike. The author wins because our predictions keep us interested in the writing. The reader wins because making predictions helps keep us focused on the action, which, in turn, makes the reading process more enjoyable.

➤ Ray Bradbury is an expert at encouraging readers to make predictions. He writes stories that are short, suspenseful, and filled with out-of-this-world creatures, places, inventions, and ideas. These elements work together to make for exciting plots that keep readers guessing.

➤ In "All Summer in a Day," Bradbury begins building suspense (and encouraging predictions) from the very first line of the text. When the story opens, we don't know who is speaking and what the speaker is getting ready for. We immediately begin guessing and predicting.

➤ As they read the first part of Bradbury's story, students should note each prediction that occurs to them. Explain that making predictions that turn out to be correct is not as important as making predictions that help you focus on the action of the story.

FOR DISCUSSION AND REFLECTION

➤ What are the different kinds of predictions we make as we read? (We make predictions about plot, characters, story outcomes, and so on.)

➤ How can these predictions affect our feelings about the story? (Our predictions keep us interested and engaged. They add to our enjoyment of a story.)

Writing

QUICK ASSESS

Do students' paragraphs:

✓ thoughtfully continue the story?

✓ reflect the style of the original?

After making predictions about what they think will happen next, students will write several paragraphs to continue the story.

READING AND WRITING EXTENSIONS

➤ Have students think about another science fiction story they enjoyed reading. Ask them to retell half of the story to the class and then invite predictions about the ending.

➤ Ask students to think of another writer they consider suspenseful and then put together a classroom library of suspense writers. Invite students to write a summary card for each book.

TWO Reading Between the Lines

Critical Reading

FOCUS
All readers draw conclusions from the evidence provided in the text.

BACKGROUND
You'll probably find that making inferences is the reading essential students find most intimidating. What a lot of readers don't realize is that they make inferences automatically as they read. Every time you say to yourself that one character is mean or another one is unfair, you are making inferences.

➤ A good many of the inferences we make are about the characters in a story. Invite students to think, for example, of the many different inferences they can make about the characters in "All Summer in a Day."

➤ Notice the complexity of Bradbury's two main characters, Margot and William. It's hard to view either of these two children with just one lens. William is naughty, for example, but he is also a child who has never seen the sun.

FOR DISCUSSION AND REFLECTION
➤ Why doesn't Margot want to be friends with the other children? (Answers will vary. She is standoffish, shy, and can't relate to the other children.)

➤ Why do William and the other children lock Margot in the closet? (Answers may include that they are bullies and are envious.)

➤ Do you sympathize with William, Margot, or both? Why? (Responses will vary. Remind students to support their opinions with evidence from the story.)

Writing

QUICK ASSESS
Do students' journal entries:

✓ reflect the point of view of either Margot or William?

✓ offer reactions to the day that are in keeping with what they know about the character?

Students are asked to imagine they are either Margot or William and then write a journal entry explaining their reactions to the day the sun came out. Before they begin, have students review their earlier predictions and look again at the inferences they made about the characters.

READING AND WRITING EXTENSIONS
➤ As an additional challenge, have students imagine they are the teacher in "All Summer in a Day" and write a journal entry describing the children as they opened the closet door.

➤ Ask students to imagine that they are the principal at Margot and William's school. Have them write a letter home to William's parents explaining the events of the day and the action the school disciplinary committee plans to take.

Three Managing the Main Idea

Critical Reading

FOCUS

The main idea of a work is its underlying meaning.

BACKGROUND

"Managing the Main Idea" introduces students to a simple equation they can use to find the main idea of a piece of nonfiction. Since most students will have no trouble finding the subject or topic of the writing, they'll need only to decide what the author has to say about that subject or topic to discover the author's main idea.

➤ "It's All in How You Say It" provides an interesting lesson to readers as well as a clearly stated and well-supported main idea. According to Roberts, white people's ignorance of Native American culture and values is a form of bigotry that is hurtful and impossible to ignore.

➤ Roberts supports her main idea by describing two incidents. In both cases, she was wounded by an outsider's ignorance of her people. She also explains that when she told her father about her pain, he told her to pay no attention to the ignorance of others, that "the outside world did not always understand Indian people." Roberts, however, finds it impossible to follow her father's advice. She is angry and hurt and feels it is important to tell others how she feels.

FOR DISCUSSION AND REFLECTION

➤ How is a main idea different from the topic or subject of a work? (The main idea is what the author has to say about the subject. It is the focus of the work.)

➤ Why is it important to understand the main idea of a work? (The main idea of a piece is usually the message the author has for his or her readers.)

➤ What does the man mean by "professional Indians?" (Responses will vary, but students should explain why Roberts and her companions might be distressed by the comment and its emphasis on costume and showmanship.)

Writing

QUICK ASSESS

Do students' narratives:

✔ clearly express a main idea?

✔ support the main idea with details, facts, or examples?

✔ include information about how the incident made students feel?

Students are asked to write about a time they felt misunderstood. As a prewriting activity, they'll use a main idea equation to help them come up with a focus for their piece.

READING AND WRITING EXTENSIONS

➤ Ask students to write a letter to Mickey Roberts explaining why they do or do not agree with her main idea. Suggest that they also discuss what they might have done had they been confronted with the same difficulties experienced by Roberts.

➤ Have students write and illustrate a book for young children entitled *It's All in How You Say It*. They can use Roberts's main idea as a starting point, but they should devote most of the book to their own ideas about respecting different cultures.

Four Author's Purpose

Critical Reading

FOCUS

Active readers infer the author's purpose from the language, tone, or theme of the work.

BACKGROUND

How are we supposed to know what the author's purpose for writing is if we can't actually ask him or her?

How often have you heard that question from students? What's your usual response? The fact is, most students don't understand that when we talk about author's purpose, we're not talking about one right answer. We're talking about the *inferences* a reader can make about purpose based on what the author says and how he or she says it.

➤ Begin your discussion of purpose with students by telling them that most authors write with one of four purposes in mind: to teach, persuade, entertain, or reveal thoughts and feelings. Then move on to a discussion of Felice Holman's "Holiday Dinner."

FOR DISCUSSION AND REFLECTION

➤ Would you say that one of Holman's purposes is to teach? (Answers will vary, but push students to specify possible lessons.)

➤ Why is the snore important? (Responses will vary, but should include that even such a minor—and annoying—detail is part of the cherished tradition.)

➤ How would you describe the family of the speaker in "Holiday Dinner"? (Responses may include close, loving, content, amused.)

Writing

QUICK ASSESS

Do students' responses:

✔ reflect a thoughtful understanding of Holman's purpose?

✔ discuss other forms of writing?

Students are asked to discuss how other forms of writing might have suited Holman's purpose. As a prewriting activity, they should explain their feelings about the poem in small groups.

READING AND WRITING EXTENSIONS

➤ Invite students to write a poem about a holiday dinner they remember well.

➤ Invite students to look through a newspaper or magazine and keep a tally of the articles they find with an entertainment purpose, a teaching purpose, and so on. What conclusions can they draw about the overall purpose of the magazine or newspaper?

Five Reflecting on Reading

Critical Reading

FOCUS

When you reflect on what you read, you question yourself about what you learned and how you can connect this selection to your own life or experience.

BACKGROUND

Critical readers know that evaluating a piece of writing means more than saying "this was good," or "this was bad." Evaluating means *reflecting* on what the selection means to you personally. Did the writing teach you something new? Did it give you a fresh perspective or help you rethink an old idea? Did it somehow change your view of yourself or others? Only after readers consider what the writing means to them can they consider how they feel about the quality of a piece.

➤ To help students begin the process of reflection, spend a moment or two discussing their answers to the question posed on page 38 about what they have learned from reading this selection. If students seem unsure, ask them:

- What did you learn about Felice Holman?

- What did you learn about poetry?

- What did you learn about yourself and your own experiences?

➤ Once they've thought about what they've learned from Holman's poem, ask them to discuss why they liked or disliked it.

FOR DISCUSSION AND REFLECTION

➤ How does a reader "reflect" on a text? (Students reflect by first connecting the text to their own lives and then deciding how they feel about it.)

➤ How is reflecting different from evaluating? (When readers reflect, they connect the story to their own lives. Evaluating is only a part of the process of reflecting.)

Writing

QUICK ASSESS

Do students' reflections:

✓ explain how their own experiences are or aren't similar to the one in the poem?

✓ show an understanding of the basics of "reflection"?

Before they reflect on their connection to Holman's poem, students will write a paragraph explaining what they learned from the poem. Have them share these with the class.

READING AND WRITING EXTENSIONS

➤ Ask students to thumb through their *Daybooks* to find a piece of writing they either really like or really dislike. Invite them to write a one-page "book review" in which they explain and then support their opinion.

➤ Ask students to reflect on the Bradbury story they read earlier in this unit. Have students write a paragraph in which they connect one or more aspects of Bradbury's story to their own lives.

Unit Overview

Invite students to think of short stories, novels, and poems that they remember well. Why are they so memorable? Chances are that students' answers will reflect one or more of the following story "essentials": setting, character, plot, point of view, or theme. In this unit, "Essentials of Story," students will see how master storytellers like Madeleine L'Engle, Richard Wilbur, and Roald Dahl combine these elements to create stories that entertain, touch, and amaze us— stories that are truly unforgettable.

Literature Focus

Lesson	Literature
1. A Story's Setting	**Natalie Babbitt,** from *The Search for Delicious* (Fiction)
	Madeleine L'Engle, from *A Wrinkle in Time* (Fiction)
2. A Story's Characters	**Roald Dahl,** from *Danny the Champion of the World* (Fiction)
3. A Story's Point of View	**Roald Dahl,** from *Danny the Champion of the World* (Fiction)
4. A Story's Plot	**Richard Wilbur,** "A Game of Catch" (Short Story)
5. A Story's Theme	

Reading Focus

1. A detailed setting helps readers visualize where the events of a story take place.
2. Noticing details about characters can help you "get into" a story.
3. Point of view is the angle from which a story is told. If the point of view changes, so does the story.
4. Paying attention to a story's action helps you understand its plot.
5. Readers can find deeper meaning in a story by connecting the story's theme to their own lives.

Writing Focus

1. Create a backdrop for a setting from a story.
2. Create a word picture to describe a character.
3. Rewrite a scene from another character's point of view.
4. Write a plot summary of a short story.
5. Write about an experience that relates to a story's theme.

One A Story's Setting

Critical Reading

FOCUS

The setting locates the reader in the story:

"They were standing in a sunlit field, and the air about them was moving with the delicious fragrance that comes only on the rarest of spring days . . . ."

BACKGROUND

In this lesson, students are asked to consider the function of setting. To help them think about a story's time and place, students will read excerpts from two novels known for their skillfully drawn settings.

➤ *The Search for Delicious* is an example of a story with an integral (essential) setting. Because the setting is such an important part of the action of the story (which involves a boy's search for the definition of the word *delicious*), Babbitt knows to open her book with a clear, engaging description of time and place. This story, she tells us, takes place in the "oldest days," long before people and their irritating "quarrels and supper parties." She also tells us succinctly and clearly where the story takes place—in a lovely spot near woods, mountains, and lakes.

➤ Consider also how Babbitt's tone helps establish setting. She narrates her story in the slow, melodic cadences of the Arthurian legends, thereby indicating to readers that they are in a time and place completely different from the world they know. Babbitt's sentences are as long, meandering, and unrushed as the time and place she describes.

➤ Madeleine L'Engle's *A Wrinkle in Time* provides students with another example of an integral setting. In L'Engle's story, three children set off on an adventure through time and space. This particular excerpt focuses on Meg, who has left the familiar world behind her (the "biting autumn evening"), and is delighted to find herself in a place that is warm, fragrant, and blooming.

➤ Notice how L'Engle's use of sensory language helps readers visualize the setting. L'Engle tells us what things look like, smell like, and feel like—all in order to make readers feel a part of her story.

FOR DISCUSSION AND REFLECTION

➤ Why do readers need to know the time and place of a story? (Readers need to be oriented to time and place before they can follow the action of the story.)

➤ What makes a setting memorable? (Answers will vary. Ask students to discuss what seems memorable about Babbitt's and L'Engle's stories.)

Writing

QUICK ASSESS

Do students' backdrops:

✔ show creativity?

✔ demonstrate an understanding of the two settings?

As students create a backdrop for a school production of Babbitt's or L'Engle's stories, stress how setting can reveal much about the mood of a story.

READING AND WRITING EXTENSIONS

➤ Ask whether students prefer L'Engle's or Babbitt's setting. Have them write a short opinion statement, analyzing particular details that appeal to them.

➤ Ask students to think about some other short story or novel settings they consider memorable. Have them write a paragraph describing why the setting is so striking. Create a class list of the characteristics mentioned.

TWO A Story's Characters

Critical Reading

FOCUS

Authors use a variety of methods to show what characters are like:

"You might think, if you didn't know him well, that he was a stern and serious man."

BACKGROUND

In this lesson, students will be asked to consider how writers create interesting, believable characters. The excerpt from Roald Dahl's *Danny the Champion of the World* works well because the narrator—who is also one of the main characters of the story—is himself one of the more memorable characters in contemporary children's literature.

➤ What students should notice first about Dahl's characters is how strongly Danny feels about the person he describes. He clearly adores everything about his father. He thinks he's fun and funny (an "eye-smiler"), talented (". . . he was a marvelous storyteller"), and creative. He loves his father so much, in fact, that he concludes it is "impossible" to say how he feels about him—even though he has just told the reader exactly how he feels.

➤ An interesting aspect of this excerpt is that all the while Danny is describing his father to the reader, the reader is also making inferences about Danny—what he looks like, how he acts, what he likes and dislikes. Danny is a remarkable character because it is so easy to empathize with him, this child who loves a parent with so much devotion. As readers, we can't help but wonder what can go wrong with this idyllic picture.

FOR DISCUSSION AND REFLECTION

➤ What makes a character interesting or memorable? (Answers will vary. Students might mention the character's personality, appearance, actions, or conversation.)

➤ Why is it important for a story to have interesting characters? (Interesting characters make it easier to connect to the action of the story and hold the attention of the reader.)

➤ What kind of a man does Danny's father seem to be? (Answers will vary. He seems loving and caring, creative, sincere, and intent.)

Writing

QUICK ASSESS

Do students' word pictures:

✓ show creativity?

✓ accurately describe Danny's father?

Before students make a word picture of Danny's father, have them make a list of words that describe him. Suggest that they reread the excerpt before they begin.

READING AND WRITING EXTENSIONS

➤ Have students write physical descriptions of Danny and his father. How do they picture these two characters?

➤ Ask students to imagine they are the father. Then have them write a brief paragraph in which the father describes his feelings for his son.

Three A Story's Point of View

Critical Reading

FOCUS

Point of view is the perspective from which a story is told.

BACKGROUND

In Lesson Three, students will consider the importance of point of view. By the time they finish the lesson, they should understand that when the point of view of a story changes, so does the story. Students will read a second excerpt from *Danny the Champion of the World* and then reflect on how the narrator's point of view affects the story.

➤ This excerpt provides students with some more information about Danny and his father, in addition to reinforcing what we already know from the previous excerpt. For example, we now know for sure that Danny is an observant, affectionate child who aims to please. We know that the father is equally observant, in addition to being a patient and loving parent.

➤ Notice the differences between this passage and the one in Lesson Two. In the first selection, the narrator's attention was directed toward his father. He described his father in some detail and then went on to describe the imaginary world that his father tells stories about. In this excerpt, Danny describes a day of kite flying with his father. As the events of the day unfold, we gain more insights into what these two characters are like.

FOR DISCUSSION AND REFLECTION

➤ From whose point of view is *Danny the Champion of the World* told? (The story is told from Danny's point of view.)

➤ Why is it important for the reader to understand a story's point of view? (Readers need to know who is describing the action in order to judge how reliable the description is. Analyzing why a writer chose a certain point of view is a key part of understanding the author's intentions.)

➤ Ask students if they know anyone like Danny's father. (As they respond, be sure they understand what Danny means when he describes his father as "too sparky" to be around.)

Writing

QUICK ASSESS

Do students' retellings:

✔ maintain the point of view of Danny's father?

✔ reflect changes required by an adult viewpoint?

Students are asked to retell the kite-flying scene from the father's point of view. As they begin, remind them to use an adult vocabulary.

READING AND WRITING EXTENSIONS

➤ To further explore point of view, have students look through their books for another selection that has a clear point of view. Encourage them to rewrite a scene from the selection from the point of view of one of the other characters.

➤ Encourage students to read the rest of *Danny the Champion of the World* and then write an explanation of how their perceptions of Danny and the father change once they know the entire story.

Four A Story's Plot

Critical Reading

FOCUS

Examining the plot of a story helps a reader understand the story's meaning.

BACKGROUND

Although character, point of view, and setting are all important to a story, most readers can't become involved in a story unless the plot is interesting. What makes for an interesting or exciting plot? The best plots are the ones that strike a balance between conflict, tension, and action. These are the plots that can hold a reader's attention through the entire story. To help set the mood for Lesson Four, you might want to ask students to make a list of stories and books that have really great plots.

➤ "A Game of Catch" is the kind of story that has wide appeal because almost everyone, at one time or another, has had experience dealing with a pest or a bully. The plot of "A Game of Catch" follows a building-block structure that students should have no trouble tracking. In his story, Wilbur lays one event (or block) upon another, building slowly but surely to the story's climax.

➤ Before they begin reading "A Game of Catch," students are asked to look at the plot mountain in their books and then make notes about the plot parts as they read the story. Students' answers will vary, but most will agree that the exposition ends after paragraph 1; that the climax is paragraphs 38 and 39 (beginning with "'I *want*—' Scho screamed as he fell"); and that the resolution is in the last paragraph of the story.

FOR DISCUSSION AND REFLECTION

➤ What kinds of plots are most interesting? (Ask students to support their different opinions and give examples if they can.)

➤ How do readers feel as the action is rising in "A Game of Catch"? (Responses will vary but should reflect the tension and suspense that builds right before the climax.)

➤ How do readers feel immediately after Scho falls (the climax)? (Responses will vary but should reflect a sense of release or resolution.)

Writing

QUICK ASSESS

Do students' responses:

✔ accurately reflect the five parts of the plot?

✔ effectively summarize the plot?

Students are asked to create a plot mountain for "A Game of Catch" and then write a plot summary.

READING AND WRITING EXTENSIONS

➤ Ask students to rewrite one of the five parts (see the plot mountain) of Wilbur's plot. After they've written their scenes, have them get together in small groups to compare their rewrites.

➤ Ask students to imagine that "A Game of Catch" is the first chapter in a book about Glennie, Monk, and Scho. Have them write a one-page outline that lists the titles of the remaining chapters and provides a brief description of each.

Five A Story's Theme

C r i t i c a l   R e a d i n g

FOCUS

To understand theme, readers must look carefully at what the author says and how he or she says it.

BACKGROUND

Students often equate "theme" with "moral." A theme is not supposed to be instructional, however. It is the meaning that an author has for readers. The reader can choose to agree with, disagree with, or even ignore it.

➤ The primary theme of a story is usually the element that holds the narrative together and gives the story its broader meaning. In "A Game of Catch," Wilbur explores one primary theme and many secondary themes. His primary theme involves the complex subject of alienation. He shows readers that when you deliberately set yourself apart—as Scho does—your feelings of isolation can be mentally, emotionally, and even physically debilitating.

➤ In addition to the primary theme of alienation, there are also several minor themes in "A Game of Catch." For example, you might discuss with students Wilbur's theme of cruelty and how a child's code of conduct is different from an adult's. You might also help students consider themes related to loneliness, peer pressure, growing up, and empathy.

FOR DISCUSSION AND REFLECTION

➤ Why do readers need to understand an author's theme? (Readers interpret the theme of a work so that they can understand the author's message and appreciate how the plot, setting, characters, and point of view are related.)

➤ How is theme different from a moral or a lesson? (A theme is not meant to be instructional. It is a message that readers can choose to agree with or disagree with.)

➤ What did Wilbur want readers to learn from this story? (Responses will vary. Students may believe Wilbur wants his readers to realize the value of friendship.)

W r i t i n g

QUICK ASSESS

Do students' descriptions:

✔ describe a learning experience of their own?

✔ explain how that experience affected them personally?

Students are asked to connect the story's theme to their own lives by writing about an experience from which they learned something. As a prewriting activity, have them consider what Scho learned from his experiences with Monk and Glennie.

READING AND WRITING EXTENSIONS

➤ Ask students to write about a short story or novel they've read that explores the theme of growing up. Did they identify or agree with the story's theme?

➤ Invite students to make a theme chart that identifies and describes some of the themes they've encountered in selections from their *Daybooks*. After they finish, they can report their findings to the class.

UNDERSTANDING CHARACTER

Unit Overview

In "Understanding Character," students will explore and evaluate five aspects of characterization: how a character looks, acts, talks, thinks and feels, and interacts with others. In the process, students will learn some of the requirements of characterization: a character must be believable and must think and act in ways that readers will find realistic.

Literature Focus

	Lesson	Literature
1.	A Character's Appearance	**Isaac Bashevis Singer,** "Utzel and His Daughter Poverty" (Short Story)
2.	A Character's Actions	**Isaac Bashevis Singer,** "Utzel and His Daughter Poverty" (Short Story)
3.	A Character's Speech	**Paula Fox,** from *One-Eyed Cat* (Fiction)
4.	A Character's Thoughts and Feelings	**Paul Fleischman,** "Kim" from *Seedfolks* (Fiction)
5.	The Other Characters	**Barbara Nichol,** from *Beethoven Lives Upstairs* (Fiction)

Reading Focus

1. Visualizing characters helps you become involved in a story.
2. Thinking about a character's actions can help you see how the character changes over the course of the story.
3. "Listening" to what a character says helps you better understand the character.
4. Understanding how a character thinks and feels can help you understand the character's actions.
5. Paying attention to how characters react to each other can help you decide how you feel about the characters.

Writing Focus

1. Invent, describe, and then sketch a funny character for a story.
2. Imagine you are the main character and write a speech about your experiences.
3. Complete a personality profile of a character.
4. Write a journal entry in the voice of the main character.
5. Write a scene between two characters, including dialogue and descriptions.

One A Character's Appearance

Critical Reading

FOCUS

Active readers try to visualize a story's character:

"Utzel was a small man, but as his daughter Poverty grew, she spread out in all directions. She was tall, broad, and heavy. At fifteen she had to lower her head to get through the doorway."

BACKGROUND

You might begin this unit by explaining to students that a character is any living being in a story, play, or poem. A "living being" can mean a person or a personified animal or object—a dog that talks, for example, or a robot that can think and reason.

➤ Characters can be flat (a character that is not well-developed) or round (a character that the reader comes to know well). Round characters often change or grow in some way over the course of the story.

➤ In this unit, students will explore various methods of character revelation. Lesson One shows students how to make inferences about a character based on how the character looks.

➤ Encourage students to visualize each character as they read Singer's story. You might suggest that they doodle portraits in the margin as they read. They can return to their drawings after reading the second half of the selection in Lesson Two.

FOR DISCUSSION AND REFLECTION

➤ Why do authors want readers to visualize the characters they describe? (Visualizing helps the reader become involved in the story and enhances the reader's overall enjoyment of the writing.)

➤ What characters in literature do you remember mostly for their physical appearances—the way they look? (Answers will vary. Request that students support their responses.)

➤ How would you describe Utzel? (Possible answers include small, grouchy, lazy, poor, tired.)

Writing

QUICK ASSESS

Do students' creations:

✔ describe the character?

✔ include enough detail so that the character can be visualized?

✔ include a picture of the character?

Students are asked to create a funny character of their own invention and then draw a picture of him or her. Before they begin, brainstorm together a list of their favorite funny characters from literature, movies, or television.

READING AND WRITING EXTENSIONS

➤ Ask students to read another short story by Isaac Bashevis Singer and then compare that story to "Utzel and His Daughter Poverty." What similarities in characterization, tone, and writing style do students see between the two stories? Have them report orally or in writing.

➤ Ask students to predict what they think might happen to Utzel and Poverty. They can write their predictions in the margin of their *Daybooks*. After they finish Lesson Two, have them check to see if their predictions were correct.

TWO A Character's Actions

Critical Reading

FOCUS

In stories, as in life, people are often changed by their experiences.

BACKGROUND

In Lesson Two, students will explore how a character's actions can give readers clues about the character's personality. For example, if a character likes to pick on smaller or weaker people, we can make the inference that the character is a bully. If, on the other hand, a character likes to take care of others, we can infer that the character is a kind person.

➤ Students should find it easy to make inferences about Utzel and Poverty. In the first part of the story, Utzel lies in bed for most of the day and complains any time he has to get up. From his actions (or his lack of action), we can infer that Utzel is extremely lazy.

➤ In the second half of the story, both Utzel and Poverty begin to take charge of their lives. As they become more active and productive, their personalities improve. Poverty soon has friends, and the townspeople begin to treat Utzel with respect.

FOR DISCUSSION AND REFLECTION

➤ How does Utzel change? (He begins to work and stops complaining. He takes an interest in his daughter, his house, and his town.)

➤ How does Poverty change? (She begins to work also. She loses weight, changes the way she dresses, and meets the man she will marry.)

➤ Why is it important for readers to pay attention to a change in character? (Character changes can provide clues about the author's themes or underlying meanings.)

Writing

QUICK ASSESS

Do students' speeches:

✔ reflect what they know about Utzel's personality?

✔ describe how and why Utzel's behavior changed?

✔ include conclusions about what Utzel learned?

Students are asked to write a speech that Utzel might give about his experiences. Before they begin, encourage students to discuss whether or not they were surprised about the changes that take place in Utzel's and Poverty's characters.

READING AND WRITING EXTENSIONS

➤ Invite students to choose one object that they think best symbolizes the changes in Utzel or Poverty. Have them sketch the object and then write a paragraph explaining the symbolism involved.

➤ Ask students to write a limerick or funny poem that is based on "Utzel and His Daughter Poverty." When they've finished, have a class poetry reading.

Three A Character's Speech

Critical Reading

FOCUS

Dialogue can reveal much about a character's values and personality:

"'There's nothing wrong with a plain life,' Uncle Hilary said with a little smile that seemed to say there was something wrong with it."

BACKGROUND

In this lesson, students explore how a character's speech—what the character says and how he or she says it—can provide clues about his or her personality and feelings.

➤ Encourage students to take notes as they read. Explain that they'll want to pay particular attention to the speech tags that precede or follow each line of dialogue: "'Ned, do come out from under the table,' Papa said with the special patience he had when he was trying not be cross." Sometimes, what a character says is less revealing than how he or she says it.

➤ Students might also note the level of tension that exists between Ned, his father, and his uncle—even though the three are engaged in a very civilized conversation. After they've read the selection one time through, you might have students return to the piece and circle the places where one of the characters becomes offended or annoyed.

FOR DISCUSSION AND REFLECTION

➤ How can a dialogue between two characters strengthen your understanding of each character? (You can make inferences about a character's personality, likes and dislikes, and so on by "listening" to what the character says and how he or she says it.)

➤ Is Uncle Hilary smart? (Push students to turn to specifics from the story as they answer. For example, they might think Uncle Hilary is smart because he speaks well, is well-travelled, and knows a lot about other places.)

Writing

QUICK ASSESS

Do students' personality profiles:

✔ demonstrate an understanding of character?

✔ use the text to support answers?

✔ reflect attention to the story's dialogue?

Students are asked to complete a personality profile for the *One-Eyed Cat* character they find most interesting. Before they begin, have them share their reasons for why this character interests them.

READING AND WRITING EXTENSIONS

➤ Invite students to connect this selection to their own lives. Which character reminds them of themselves? Why? Have them write a journal entry explaining their choice.

➤ Have students read more of *One-Eyed Cat* or another Paula Fox novel of their choice. When they've finished reading, they can write a brief review that might be published in a classroom literary magazine.

Four A Character's Thoughts and Feelings

C r i t i c a l   R e a d i n g

FOCUS

Often readers must make inferences about what motivates a character.

BACKGROUND

In this lesson, students will explore the connection between a character's thoughts and feelings and the character's actions. Remind students that often a character's motivation is not stated directly and that they will need to "read between the lines." An important part of this lesson concerns point of view, the perspective from which a story is told. You might want to spend a moment or two reviewing point of view with students:

➤ First-person point of view: The story is narrated by the first person, or "I." The reader is privy to this person's thoughts, feelings, emotions, and actions.

➤ Omniscient point of view: The story is told from a third-person (he, she, they) perspective. The narrator is all-knowing, which means that the narrator can tell readers every detail of action, thought, and feeling.

➤ Objective or dramatic point of view: The story is again told from the third person, though no one explains to the reader what is going on or what the characters feel or think.

FOR DISCUSSION AND REFLECTION

➤ What is an inference? (An inference is any reasonable guess you can make based on the evidence or information provided.)

➤ What inferences can you make about why Kim planted the seeds? (Responses will vary, but they should focus on Kim's need to feel a sense of connection with her father.)

➤ How does Kim feel before planting the beans? (Answers may include that she is sad and hesitant.)

W r i t i n g

QUICK ASSESS

Do students' journal entries:

✓ reflect Kim's point of view?

✓ show a careful reading of the story?

Students are asked to imagine they are Kim and then write a journal entry in which she describes her emotions before, during, and after planting the lima beans.

READING AND WRITING EXTENSIONS

➤ Ask students to write a paragraph or two describing a time they felt some of the emotions that Kim experiences as she plants the beans. Remind them to show—rather than tell—how they felt.

➤ Invite students to thumb through their books or look over the classroom library to find another selection that deals with the death of a loved one. Have the student read the selection and then present it to the class. In their presentations, students can make comparisons between their selection and Fleischman's "Kim."

Five The Other Characters

Critical Reading

FOCUS

Active readers should pay attention to how characters view one another:

"Mr. Beethoven is so famous that sometimes people stop outside our house, hoping they will see him."

BACKGROUND

This lesson will help students understand how they can find clues about a character by noticing how the character looks, speaks, and acts, and by noting what other characters have to say about him or her. Help them consider if the other characters like the main character. Do the other characters show respect for the main character? Why or why not?

➤ *Beethoven Lives Upstairs* is a series of letters written from a young boy to his uncle. The boy—whose father has recently died—is at first annoyed with and then frightened by the "eccentric" Mr. Beethoven, his mother's tenant.

➤ What's most interesting about this story is the contrast Nichol sets up between the adults' view of Beethoven and Christoph's view. The adults are willing to ignore Beethoven's strangeness (after all, he is a genius), while the boy, Christoph, is truly alarmed by Beethoven's odd behavior.

➤ When they've finished reading, you might ask students which character seems the best judge of Beethoven—Christoph, Christoph's mother, or the uncle? Encourage them to explain their opinions.

FOR DISCUSSION AND REFLECTION

➤ How can a reader discover what a character is "really" like? (A reader can learn about a character by watching how the character acts, talks, and looks. The comments of other characters are also helpful in understanding character.)

➤ How do you know if one character's assessment of another character is fair or accurate? (Although you can never be completely sure, you can usually trust the character or characters whom you admire or sympathize with. For example, in Nichol's story, the reader sympathizes with Christoph and is, therefore, inclined to trust what he says about Beethoven.)

Writing

QUICK ASSESS

Do students' scenes:

✔ include descriptions of the characters' appearances and thoughts?

✔ create believable dialogue for the two characters?

Students will create a scene involving the character they created in Lesson One and a new character. They should describe how the two characters look, speak, think, and act toward each other.

READING AND WRITING EXTENSIONS

➤ Students might be surprised to discover how much they know about Uncle, Christoph, and Beethoven just from reading these short letters. Ask them to create a Venn diagram that lists as many adjectives as they can think of to describe each of the characters. Have them use the intersecting part in the middle to note characteristics that all three characters share.

➤ Invite students to finish reading *Beethoven Lives Upstairs* and then to report on the ending to the class.

Unit Overview

This unit introduces students to five of the many ingredients that go into the literary alphabet soup known as "author's craft:" similes, metaphors, personification, sensory language, and irony. As they read and respond to a fable and a variety of poetry, students will discover how each time one of these ingredients is used, the "soup"—the story, poem, or article—changes just a bit.

Literature Focus

	Lesson	Literature
1.	Surprising Comparisons	**E. E. Cummings,** "maggie and milly and molly and may" (Poetry)
2.	What It Is	**Rita Dove,** "Grape Sherbet" (Poetry)
3.	Almost Human	**Aesop,** "The Fox and the Crow" (Fable)
4.	See It, Hear It, Feel It . . .	**X.J. Kennedy,** "Telephone Talk" (Poetry)
5.	It's a Twist	**Shel Silverstein,** "Almost Perfect" (Poetry)

Reading Focus

1. Notice the ways authors use similes to help us look at familiar things in new ways.
2. Authors use metaphors to suggest new ways of seeing and understanding.
3. Authors use personification to give nonhuman things human characteristics.
4. Authors use sensory language to bring their writing to life for readers.
5. Irony is one technique authors use to add humor and depth to their writing.

Writing Focus

1. Create three or more similes that describe a favorite place, object, food, animal, or concept.
2. Complete a Venn diagram that explores a poem's metaphor.
3. Describe an object using personification.
4. Add to a poem by writing a stanza that includes images that appeal to the senses.
5. Write an analysis of how irony is used in a poem's ending.

One Surprising Comparisions

Critical Reading

FOCUS

Similes make us look at things in new ways:

"may came home with a smooth round stone / as small as a world and as large as alone."

BACKGROUND

The first type of figurative language students will learn about in this unit is simile. Unlike metaphors, similes rarely give students trouble because they are fairly easy to spot. If, however, students are unsure about whether a comparison qualifies as a simile, they can use this simple test, which involves asking two questions about the items being compared:

1. Does the comparison use a connective word such as *like, as, appears, than,* or *seems*?

2. Is it a comparison of two dissimilar things?

If the answer to both of these questions is yes, the comparison can be called a simile.

➤ In his poem "maggie and milly and molly and may," E. E. Cummings uses similes to help bring freshness and vitality to his descriptions: "may came home with a smooth round stone / as small as a world and as large as alone."

➤ The similes in the poem breathe new life into a subject that poets have been writing about forever: the sea and its power to renew and restore. For Cummings, the sea is everything that is "languid" and "smooth" and trouble-free, so that even the lost souls—"(like a you or a me)"—can find peace on the beach.

FOR DISCUSSION AND REFLECTION

➤ What is a simile? (a comparison between two basically dissimilar things that nonetheless have something in common)

➤ What are some reasons writers use similes? (Similes help create a vivid picture in the reader's mind; similes can convey a lot of information in a few words; similes can make a topic or idea seem fresh, new, and memorable.)

Writing

QUICK ASSESS

Do students' webs:

✓ include four similes?

✓ compare two unlike things?

Share some similes of your own before students try to create three or more similes that describe a food, an object, an animal, a place, or a concept.

READING AND WRITING EXTENSIONS

➤ Ask students to take one of the similes they created for the activity on page 75 and incorporate it into a poem or paragraph of their own.

➤ Invite students to illustrate a simile or other comparison E. E. Cummings makes in "maggie and milly and molly and may."

Two What It Is

Critical Reading

FOCUS
Metaphors bring freshness to writing:

"Each dollop / of sherbert, later, / is a miracle . . . ."

BACKGROUND
Like a simile, a metaphor is a comparison between two unlike things. Unlike similes, however, most metaphors don't use connective words. For this reason, students often find it more difficult to identify and interpret metaphors.

➤ "Grape Sherbet" is an excellent poem for a lesson on metaphor because it employs both easy to spot comparisons (direct metaphors) and others that are more difficult to see (implied metaphors). Begin by helping students see the metaphors Dove uses to describe the grape sherbet (grape sherbet is "swirled snow," "gelled light," and "lavender"). Also ask students to consider how these metaphors can help them see or visualize the sherbet Dad carries in his hands.

➤ Although some students may not notice it, Dove also creates a magnificent metaphor when she compares the grape sherbet to a miracle, a gift of love from a father to his children: "Each dollop / of sherbet, later, / is a miracle. . . ."

➤ Because the underlying meaning of the poem may cause difficulty for students, you might want to devote some time to discussing students' interpretations. For many readers, this is a poem that reaffirms the strength of family and the importance of family rituals like having homemade grape sherbet on Memorial Day. For others, the poem is a comment on Memorial Day and our tendency, in celebration, to ignore the day's deeper meaning: "We thought no one was lying / there under our feet."

FOR DISCUSSION AND REFLECTION
➤ How is a metaphor different from a simile? (A metaphor uses no connective words. Metaphors often make deeper or more complex comparisons.)

➤ Why do authors use metaphors? (Possible answers include to make their writing fresh, concise, and vital.)

➤ How is the grandmother a "torch / of pure refusal"? (Responses will vary.)

Writing

QUICK ASSESS
Do students' Venn diagrams:

✔ demonstrate students' understanding of metaphor?

✔ show that students have made a thoughtful analysis of Dove's poem?

Create a metaphor of your own and do a model Venn diagram on the board before students make their own to explore one of Dove's metaphors in "Grape Sherbet."

READING AND WRITING EXTENSIONS
➤ Ask students to create a list of food metaphors that are similar in style to the grape sherbet metaphor that Rita Dove creates. To start, have students brainstorm some suggestions to complete this metaphor: Cotton candy is _____.

➤ Ask students to thumb through their books, keeping an eye out for similes and metaphors in poetry and short stories. Have them note the examples they find and then present their favorites to the class.

Three Almost Human

Critical Reading

FOCUS

In animal fables, animals often personify human traits:

"A crow was sitting on a branch of a tree with a piece of cheese in her beak when a fox observed her and set his wits to work to discover some way of getting the cheese."

BACKGROUND

In "Almost Human," students explore another type of figurative language, personification. Explain to students that in personification, human qualities are attributed to nonhuman or inanimate things—animals, objects, ideas, and concepts. Most students find personification easy to spot and still easier to imitate.

➤ In "The Fox and the Crow," both animals exhibit human qualities. The fox, who can talk and reason, is wily and clever, nimbly using flattery to cajole the crow to give up her cheese. The crow, who is taken in by the fox's flattery, foolishly opens her mouth to sing and drops her cheese.

➤ Remind students that most fables, fairy tales, and folk tales use personification. In these kinds of stories, animals can talk, the moon can whisper, or "Greed" can walk around on two feet. Personification is not limited to fairy and folk tales, of course. Science fiction and fantasy also use personification. Machines that can think and reason like humans, for example, are a type of personification.

FOR DISCUSSION AND REFLECTION

➤ What is personification? (a comparison in which a nonhuman thing is given human traits)

➤ What examples of personification can be found in "The Fox and the Crow"? (The main characters are animals who talk, have feelings, and behave like human beings.)

➤ What lesson does the fable teach? (Answers may vary but should focus on resisting flattery. Remind students that in a fable the animal characters' behavior is generally a mirror to human experience.)

Writing

QUICK ASSESS

Do students' sentences:

✔ demonstrate an understanding of personification?

✔ show thought and creativity?

After they examine personification in "The Fox and the Crow," students will write a sentence assigning human qualities to an everyday object.

READING AND WRITING EXTENSIONS

➤ As a further challenge, have students develop a fable or folk tale around the object they have personified. They can model their tales on "The Fox and the Crow."

➤ Have students imagine they are the crow. Ask them to describe the encounter with the fox to a group of other animal friends.

Four See It, Hear It, Feel It . . .

Critical Reading

FOCUS

Sensory details can appeal to any of the senses, including the sense of sound:

"Give a blow in your phone, / My phone makes it thunder."

BACKGROUND

When an author uses sensory language, he or she invites the reader to step into a work and take a look around. Encourage students to think about what they see, what they hear, and what they taste, feel, and smell.

➤ In "Telephone Talk," the speaker is flat on his or her back, phone up against the ear. The reader is on the receiving end of the call. The poet's job is to make readers feel a part of the call. To accomplish this, X. J. Kennedy uses sensory language. He tells you what you might be hearing ("How would my shrill whistle / Sound to you, I wonder?"); he tells you what you might be smelling or tasting (raisin toast); and he tells you what you might be seeing (the dark night outside your window).

➤ Notice that Kennedy's poem is lovely because of its language—not because of its subject matter (two teens talking on the phone). It's an excellent example of how words can sometimes stand on their own, apart from the message, emotion, or idea they represent.

FOR DISCUSSION AND REFLECTION

➤ What is the effect of the sensory details in "Telephone Talk"? (The sensory details put the reader "there"; they bring the poem to life for the reader.)

➤ How does Kennedy appeal to your sense of sound? (Possible responses include the "munching" of bread, the whispers, the whistle, and the phone making a blow sound like thunder.)

➤ Which sensory details make "Telephone Talk" most vivid for you? (Responses will vary. Ask students to support their ideas.)

Writing

QUICK ASSESS

Do students' stanzas:

✓ include sensory language?

✓ continue the rhyme and rhythm patterns?

Students are asked to write a stanza for "Telephone Talk" that reflects their own telephone habits. Encourage them to read their creations aloud.

READING AND WRITING EXTENSIONS

➤ Ask students to rewrite Kennedy's poem leaving out all of the sensory images. How does the overall effect of the poem change?

➤ Have students write a journal entry in which they comment on Kennedy's idea that talking on the phone with a friend is "closer than when walking / down the street together."

ive It's a Twist

Critical Reading

BACKGROUND

Some writers just love to surprise us. They build suspense, get us emotionally involved, and then bang—hit us with a shocker. We react with surprise, pleasure, and sometimes even the feeling that we'd like to start back at the beginning and reread the whole story. Of course, this is exactly what the author intended.

➤ If you'd like to discuss irony with students, you might begin by explaining that in literature, there are three different types of irony:

- verbal irony: words that imply the opposite of what they literally mean

- irony of situation: things that turn out completely differently than expected

- dramatic irony: a situation when the reader or audience knows more than the characters do

➤ You might also tell students that when they see irony in a piece of writing, they can usually assume that the irony masks an important message from the author.

➤ The last lines of "Almost Perfect" provide students with a clear example of irony of situation. In this case, the irony of situation masks Silverstein's larger comment or criticism of most people's tendency to be dissatisfied with their lot in life. Instead of accepting what we have, many of us spend our time waiting for something better.

FOR DISCUSSION AND REFLECTION

➤ Why do writers use irony? (to add humor or a sense of surprise to the writing)

➤ How is irony different from humor? (Irony often serves as a way to make a thought-provoking insight about human beings or about life.)

➤ In what situations have you criticized something or someone as "almost perfect . . . but not quite"? (Responses will vary.)

Writing

As students begin to explain what's ironic about the last part of Silverstein's poem, review with them how irony of situation works. Have them articulate what they think are common expectations of heaven.

READING AND WRITING EXTENSIONS

➤ Ask students to return to "The Fox and the Crow" in Lesson Three. What irony do they find in this tale? Have them explain in a paragraph or two.

➤ Invite students to turn "Almost Perfect" into a short, short story—one page or less. Remind them to offer plenty of description and to try for an ironic twist.

Unit Overview

This unit helps students to understand the construction of an argument and to recognize how individual parts of an argument come together to persuade a reader or an audience. In "The Art of Argument," students will learn to read and reflect on the argument's main idea and supporting details. They will also explore how and why writers include opposing viewpoints. And—perhaps most importantly—they'll learn some techniques that can help them thoughtfully evaluate any argument.

Literature Focus

	Lesson	Literature
1.	What's It All About?	**Steve Forbes,** "A Uniformly Good Idea" (Nonfiction)
2.	With Good Reason	
3.	Seeing the Other Side	**Rosa Velasquez,** from "Robots Will Never Replace Humans" (Nonfiction)
4.	That's a Fact!	
5.	Good Point?	**Robert R. Halpern,** from *Green Planet Rescue* (Nonfiction-Science)

Reading Focus

1. Finding the main idea of an argument helps you understand the writer's viewpoint.
2. Writers use details and reasons to support the main idea of an argument.
3. Writers include (and refute) opposing viewpoints to strengthen their own.
4. Looking for facts will help you decide if an argument is a convincing one.
5. To evaluate an argument, look for details and facts that support the opinion.

Writing Focus

1. Write a letter to the editor explaining your perspective on an issue.
2. Use details to support an argument.
3. Write a paragraph that refutes opposing arguments.
4. Make a list of facts that support an opinion.
5. Write a proposal that presents your views on a local issue.

One What's It All About?

Critical Reading

FOCUS

Forbes's main idea is that "uniforms underscore that the purpose of school is learning, not making fashion statements."

BACKGROUND

Before beginning this lesson, students might benefit from a brief introduction to argument. In a written argument, the author makes an assertion and then attempts to do one of two things: change the reader's opinion about an issue or topic or convince the reader to take action. Remind students that for an argument to be effective, the writer must provide readers with an assertion or main idea that is strong and clearly worded. The writer then must back it up with evidence that appeals to readers' emotions, intellect, or both.

➤ Steve Forbes's "A Uniformly Good Idea" follows the classic structure for an argument. It begins with an assertion, works to support the assertion, acknowledges and refutes opposing arguments, and finishes by restating the viewpoint.

➤ Students will probably have no trouble finding Forbes's main idea, especially since it is the first sentence of the piece. Notice how Forbes carefully reminds readers of his main idea—his assertion—at the beginning of each new paragraph. This technique of stating and restating the original assertion helps readers stay focused on the writer's intent.

FOR DISCUSSION AND REFLECTION

➤ What is viewpoint in an argument? (The writer's viewpoint is his or her position on the issue or topic presented.)

➤ What is Forbes's main idea in the article? (School uniforms are a good idea. They can help students become better learners.)

Writing

QUICK ASSESS

Do students' letters:

✓ express a clear opinion?

✓ appeal to both emotions and intellect?

Before students begin to write a letter to the editor expressing their viewpoints on school uniforms, initiate a class discussion on the topic.

READING AND WRITING EXTENSIONS

➤ Ask students to work in small groups to come up with a list titled "Top Ten Reasons Why School Uniforms Are/Are Not A Good Idea." When they've finished, ask each group to present their list to the class.

➤ Have students write up a plan for a short story that explores the debate about school uniforms. Have them make a list of characters, describe the setting, and give an outline or brief summary of the plot.

Two **With Good Reason**

Critical Reading

FOCUS

An argument is only as good as its supporting details.

BACKGROUND

Begin this lesson by reminding students that every argument needs support. There are several different ways to support an argument. A writer can support his or her viewpoint by calling on personal experiences, the experiences of others, or authoritative sources. The most effective arguments will use a combination of two or more types of support.

➤ In "With Good Reason," students are asked to consider the details Forbes offers to support his assertion in "A Uniformly Good Idea." Although Forbes's argument is short, he manages to thoroughly back up his claim.

➤ Most of his supporting details draw on the experience of others: "Too many students spend an inordinate amount of time worrying about what they should wear." In fact, Forbes's main idea—"Schools across the country should follow the example of Long Beach, Calif., which is requiring public school students to wear uniforms"— makes it clear that it is the experience of others (Long Beach schools) that helped him formulate his argument.

FOR DISCUSSION AND REFLECTION

➤ What is the purpose of supporting details in an argument? (They are used to back up the author's main idea.)

➤ What is the effect if the writer does not support his or her main idea? (Answers will vary. Students should note that the author's argument will likely be weak or ineffective without supporting details.)

➤ Which of Forbes's supporting details are the most persuasive? (Responses will vary.)

Writing

QUICK ASSESS

Do students' notes:

✔ clearly state their main idea?

✔ include a range of effective supporting details?

Students are asked to support an argument of their own in a note to their parents. Help them choose a topic by brainstorming a list of possibilities together on the board.

READING AND WRITING EXTENSIONS

➤ Invite students to find an example of persuasive writing in their *Daybooks*, a newspaper, or a magazine. Have them read the piece and then create a main idea and supporting details web similar to the one they completed for "A Uniformly Good Idea."

➤ Ask students to imagine that Forbes is coming to their school to speak to parents and students about school uniforms. What questions would students like to ask him? What comments would they like to make? Have them make a list of their questions and ideas.

Three Seeing the Other Side

Critical Reading

FOCUS

Effective arguments acknowledge opposing viewpoints.

BACKGROUND

The most skillful persuasive writers know how important it is to acknowledge opposing arguments. Explain to students that when writers include a discussion of opposing viewpoints, they show themselves to be rational, reasonable people who have carefully considered the many different sides of the argument. As a result, the argument is more convincing.

➤ There are many different ways to refute opposing arguments. The most common method is to briefly acknowledge (restate) the opposing argument and then explain why the argument is false, flawed, or foolish. For example, Forbes carefully summarizes what the "critics" have to say—"Perverse-minded critics carp that such dress codes will lessen youngsters' individuality"—and then quickly refutes this view by saying, "Hogwash. Kids will learn that they can distinguish themselves in more substantive ways. . . ."

➤ In "Robots Will Never Replace Humans," Rosa Velasquez shows that she has considered both sides of the argument. She begins by presenting her viewpoint that robots are not, and will never be, sophisticated enough to replace human beings. Later, however, she acknowledges that robots can be useful for certain lower-level tasks, such as building car bodies and stacking boxes for shipping.

FOR DISCUSSION AND REFLECTION

➤ Why is it important to present opposing arguments? (to show your readers that you've examined all sides of an issue)

➤ What are some ways that writers counter opposing viewpoints? (Writers can use their own experiences, the experiences of others, or facts and statistics to show that the opposing viewpoint is wrong.)

Writing

QUICK ASSESS

Do students' paragraphs:

✓ present strong arguments for their side?

✓ acknowledge and then refute the opposition?

Students will review the note they wrote to their parents in Lesson Two and then consider ways to refute opposing viewpoints. Having them work in pairs will help sharpen their thinking on their issues.

READING AND WRITING EXTENSIONS

➤ Have students imagine they've been asked by a scientific research firm to write an article entitled "Humans Need Robots." Working in small groups, students can brainstorm ideas for the article, including ways to refute opposing arguments.

➤ Ask students to write about a science fiction movie, book, or television show that involves robots. What are the robots like? Are they all "smart" and "well behaved"?

Four That's a Fact!

Critical Reading

FOCUS

Facts can be proven to be true or false:

"That creature, however, simply doesn't exist in the real world."

BACKGROUND

Sometimes students have trouble understanding the role that facts can play in an argument. You might begin this lesson by explaining that although the writer's viewpoint or assertion is considered an opinion, the writer can and should use facts to support that opinion.

➤ In "Robots Will Never Replace Humans," Velasquez moves smoothly from opinion to fact and back to opinion again. Each opinion she offers (for example, that robots "have their place") is supported by at least one fact (that robots "can perform certain tasks, such as building car bodies in factories and stacking boxes for shipping"). At other points in the essay, she offers a fact first (that "even a baby less than two years old can do three things no robot can: recognize a face, understand a human language, and walk on two legs") and then follows with an opinion that relates to the fact (that "if they can't do everything a person can, then robots will never replace humans").

FOR DISCUSSION AND REFLECTION

➤ What's a fact? (something that can be proven true or false)

➤ What's an opinion? (something that someone believes is true but cannot be proven true or false)

➤ How effective are the facts Velasquez presents? What additional facts would be persuasive? (Responses will vary.)

➤ Are robots smarter than babies? (Responses will vary.)

Writing

QUICK ASSESS

Do students' responses:

✔ make a clear statement of opinion?

✔ list facts to support their opinions?

Students are asked to support an opinion of their own. As a prewriting activity, have the class discuss the facts and opinions they highlighted in Velasquez's article.

READING AND WRITING EXTENSIONS

➤ Ask students to think about or research what robots can do. Are there robots who can "recognize a face, understand a human language, and walk on two legs?" Have students explain what they know and encourage them to share as many facts as they can with the class.

➤ Invite students to read a science fiction short story or novel that includes at least one robot as a character. When they've finished, have them review the story for the class.

Five Good Point?

Critical Reading

FOCUS

When you evaluate an argument, you decide how convincing it is.

BACKGROUND

Once students understand the persuasive techniques a writer uses, they are ready to begin evaluating the argument. Remind students that evaluating an argument does not involve agreeing or disagreeing with the assertion. Evaluating an argument means judging its validity. Has the author made a reasonable assertion? Is the assertion well-supported? These are some of the questions critical readers ask when they read a persuasive piece.

➤ In this lesson, students are asked to read and evaluate an excerpt from *Green Planet Rescue*. In this selection, Robert R. Halpern takes on the task of convincing readers that we need to be concerned about the "20,000 to 25,000 of the plant species on Earth that are endangered, vulnerable, or rare." He begins with a nod to the opposition ("Plants just grow, don't they? Weeds sprout in every open space, so what's the problem?") and then goes on to explain that we should worry because these plants are important.

➤ Notice that Halpern provides strong and varied support for his argument. He uses facts ("They produce the basic resources for life on Earth") and emotional appeals ("Can we afford to find out what life without a particular species would be like?") to add strength and substance to his claim.

FOR DISCUSSION AND REFLECTION

➤ What are the criteria for a good argument? (It must be clear, logical, and well supported. The best arguments acknowledge and then refute opposing viewpoints.)

➤ Why is it important to evaluate each argument you come across? (Deciding whether an argument is logical and thorough will help you decide whether you agree or disagree with the argument's main points.)

➤ How good an argument does Halpern make? (Responses will vary.)

Writing

QUICK ASSESS

Do students' proposals:

✓ state a clear opinion on a local issue?

✓ include facts to support the opinion?

✓ acknowledge opposing viewpoints?

Students are asked to use the strategies they've learned to write a proposal that makes an argument about a local issue. Have the class brainstorm a list of possible topics.

READING AND WRITING EXTENSIONS

➤ As an additional challenge, ask students to return to the Forbes and Velasquez articles and evaluate each of the arguments. Which is stronger? Why? What are some suggestions for improvement?

➤ Invite students to find an interesting editorial in a newspaper and magazine. Have them read and then report on the different parts of the writer's argument: the main ideas, the supporting details, the opposing viewpoints, and so on.

Unit Overview

In this unit, students are invited to explore the life and literature of Newbery award-winning author Lois Lowry, a keen observer and recorder of events. Using a "slice-of-life" writing style, Lowry writes about "real" young people and the issues and problems that concern them. As a result, Lowry's books hold enormous appeal for young readers, most of whom find it easy to identify with her characters, story lines, and themes.

Literature Focus

Lesson	Literature
1. Writing from Experience	from *A Summer to Die* (Fiction)
2. Tackling Tough Issues	from *A Summer to Die* (Fiction)
3. Painting a Picture	from *Autumn Street* (Fiction)
4. Making History Come Alive	from *Number the Stars* (Historical Fiction)
5. Where Do Stories Come From?	from Newbery acceptance speech (Nonfiction)

Reading Focus

1. Writers draw on experiences and relationships in their own lives to create realistic characters and situations in their stories.

2. Writers tackle tough issues to show that there are lessons that can be learned from difficult situations.

3. Focus on details as you read to create mental pictures of the setting and learn about characters.

4. Writers of historical fiction blend events that happened in history with fictional details to make history come "alive."

5. Writers use many different sources, such as interviews and photographs, when they create works of historical fiction.

Writing Focus

1. Use a Venn diagram to explore sibling relationships.

2. List ideas for personal narratives.

3. Make a web about place, including descriptive details, to convey your overall feeling about it.

4. Explain your feelings about a story in a letter to Lowry.

5. Write Lowry's "recipe" for creating historical fiction.

One Writing from Experience

C r i t i c a l   R e a d i n g

FOCUS

Authors who write from experience help readers connect to what they read.

BACKGROUND

Almost any writer will tell you that it's best to "stick to what you know"—that is, to write from your own life and experiences. Newbery medal-winning author Lois Lowry has clearly taken this advice to heart. In almost every book she writes, the reader gets glimpses of people Lowry has known, places she's lived, or events from her own life. Because she borrows material from her own life, Lowry's stories have a "genuine" feel to them that young people find highly appealing.

➤ In *A Summer to Die*, Lowry explores the difficult subject of the death of a family member without the sentimentality found in most books for young readers. Lowry's tone, while sympathetic, is straightforward and no-nonsense. She has experience dealing with this issue and intends to share her wisdom with her readers.

➤ What students might find most interesting is that Molly's sickness is not the sole focus of Lowry's narrative. Lowry also explores Meg's feelings about herself, her family, and her friends. Life goes on, Lowry says, even to the point that two sisters (one of whom is gravely ill) can still fight about whose side of the room a pair of sneakers belongs on.

FOR DISCUSSION AND REFLECTION

➤ Why do writers like to draw from their own experiences for material? (Responses may include that when they use their own experiences, their stories feel more realistic.)

➤ How is writing what you know different from writing an autobiography? (When you write what you know, you insert real experiences into a fictional narrative. Autobiography is considered completely nonfiction.)

➤ What specific incidents in Lowry's writing strike you as realistic? (Responses will vary, but you should push students to explain their choices.)

W r i t i n g

QUICK ASSESS

Do students' Venn diagrams:

✓ express understanding of Molly and Meg's relationship?

✓ connect Lowry's sisters to another pair of siblings?

Students are asked to describe the relationship between Molly and Meg and then use a Venn diagram to compare the sisters' relationships to that of another pair of siblings.

READING AND WRITING EXTENSIONS

➤ Invite students to read all of *A Summer to Die* and then write a book report or book review that they can present to the class.

➤ Have students remember and write about a time when someone they cared about was ill.

Two Tackling Tough Issues

Critical Reading

FOCUS

Stories help us make sense of the world around us:

"He swallowed hard and said, 'Dying is a very solitary thing.'"

BACKGROUND

In *A Summer to Die*, Lowry juggles several tough issues—a child's death, sibling rivalry, family relationships, and boy-girl relationships. In this story (and in many of her stories), Lowry makes the point that human connections are rarely simple and never easy. They are multidimensional and at any given moment can be comprised of grief, jealousy, joy, anger, elation, and pettiness. These emotions, Lowry says, are all a part of growing up.

FOR DISCUSSION AND REFLECTION

➤ Why do you think an author would want to write about a difficult issue, such as death? (Students might suggest that writers want readers to learn something from reading about difficult topics. Accept other reasonable responses.)

➤ What do you think Lowry hopes readers will learn from *A Summer to Die*? (Responses will vary. Ask students to explain their answers.)

➤ Why does the father tell Meg that "Dying is a very solitary thing?" (Responses will vary but may include that he wants Meg to realize that the family can do no more for Molly than show her love through their presence.)

➤ Would you find Meg's father's words comforting if you were in her situation? (Students' opinions will vary. Help them understand that by verbalizing the circumstances, the father may also be calming his own fears.)

Writing

QUICK ASSESS

Do students' responses:

✓ fill their banks with a range of problems or situations?

✓ indicate which experiences they'd most like to write about?

Students are asked to create an "experience bank" of problems or situations that they could draw upon for their own writing. Advise them to try to balance positive and negative expectations.

READING AND WRITING EXTENSIONS

➤ Ask students to list some of the issues that today's teens seem bothered by. You might lead a discussion about different ways to cope with some of these issues. Later, students can write about their reactions to the discussion.

➤ Lowry often writes realistic fiction. Find out what other realistic fiction students have read and enjoyed. Ask them to put together a class reading list that they can use for outside or free reading.

Three Painting a Picture

Critical Reading

FOCUS

Lowry uses details to help readers visualize what she describes:

"In the sky, the painted ghosts would flutter, hovering like Chagall angels …."

BACKGROUND

In many ways, *Autumn Street* is a departure from Lowry's normal fare. Though it's not fantasy, it's probably as close to fantasy as a realistic writer ever gets. In this story Lowry focuses her attention on her craft. She uses similes ("the clipped lawn as smooth and green as patchwork pockets on a velvet skirt") and metaphors ("Even today, with a brush, I would blur the woods") as a way of showing her love for language. Through vivid images, sensory details, and precise description, Lowry creates a picture with language.

➤ Students might benefit from a close analysis of a passage or two. Though Lowry's style in *Autumn Street* is artistic, it is never flowery. Encourage students to explore Lowry's figurative language and her sensory images: for example, "the rough pink brick" or "gauzy dresses that billowed."

FOR DISCUSSION AND REFLECTION

➤ Why are details important? (They give the work focus and help the reader visualize the person, place, or thing described. They also function as support for the theme or main idea.)

➤ What happens if a writer doesn't use enough detail? (Responses may vary, but students may say that the work is dull, hard to connect with.)

➤ Why does Lowry leave some details "blurry?" (Responses will vary.)

Writing

QUICK ASSESS

Do students' webs:

✓ include a range of details?

✓ suggest an overall feeling about the place?

Before students draw a sketch of *Autumn Street*, urge them to review the details they circled and underlined. Examining Lowry's details will help students to create a web that shows a place that has been important to them.

READING AND WRITING EXTENSIONS

➤ Ask students to write a short story—or the opening for a short story—that is set in the place they used for their webs. Remind them to include plenty of details.

➤ Have students thumb through excerpts from *A Summer to Die*, looking for striking details. Ask them to read aloud from the piece and then to explain why it appeals to them.

Four Making History Come Alive

Critical Reading

FOCUS

Historical fiction mixes real events with fictional details:

"They plan to arrest all the Danish Jews. They plan to take them away. And we have been told that they may come tonight."

BACKGROUND

Most critics would say that *Number the Stars* is Lowry's most impressive work. The beauty of the novel lies in the simple, dignified manner in which Lowry portrays this horrifying episode of history.

➤ In this novel (and in many of her other works), Lowry creates a realistic balance between major problems and minor irritations. For example, although there's a frightening war going on, blackened shoes, stories about kings and queens, and chicken for dinner are also important—at least to the children of the story.

➤ Make sure that students recognize that Lowry's story is told primarily from the viewpoint of a child. Because of this, readers are given a glimpse of history not usually offered in the history books.

FOR DISCUSSION AND REFLECTION

➤ What is historical fiction? (a blend of historical facts and events with made-up details)

➤ Why is historical fiction so popular with children? (Answers will vary. Invite students to discuss examples of historical fiction they have enjoyed.)

➤ Do you like Lowry's mix of fact and fiction? (Responses will vary.)

Writing

QUICK ASSESS

Do students' letters:

✓ explain their reactions to the selection?

✓ use details from the selection to support what they say?

✓ use correct letter form?

Students are asked to write a letter to Lois Lowry explaining how the selection from *Number the Stars* made them feel. Encourage them to refer to specific passages.

READING AND WRITING EXTENSIONS

➤ Invite students to compare the selection from *Number the Stars* to a selection from *Autumn Street* or *A Summer to Die*. Does Lowry's writing style stay fairly consistent? What similarities and differences do students see?

➤ Invite students to speak with a family member or neighbor about his or her recollections of World War II. What do they remember most? Why? Once again, students can share what they find with the class.

Five Where Do Stories Come From?

Critical Reading

FOCUS

Lois Lowry on her methods of research:

"In Denmark I collected countless details to add to those that Annelise and Kirsten told me of their own lives."

BACKGROUND

In "Where Do Stories Come From?" students have the chance to see how the several different "parts" of Lowry's style as a writer come together. First and foremost, Lowry is a realist. She sets out to show readers what it was like to be a child in Copenhagen during the German occupation. How did the Jews feel? How did King Christian X feel? How did the little children feel? These are just a few of the questions Lowry is determined to answer in her novel. She is a reporter "assigned" to present the facts of the story.

➤ Lowry is also a storyteller, however, which is why she doesn't hesitate to use symbolism ("the high shiny boots") or other literary techniques to flesh out her story.

➤ After they've finished reading Lowry's speech, students might enjoy returning to the excerpt from *Number the Stars*. Have them discuss whether their views of the story changed after learning about Lowry's intentions.

FOR DISCUSSION AND REFLECTION

➤ Why do writers need to do research before writing? (so that the information they present is accurate and realistic)

➤ What are some of the different sources Lowry used to research *Number the Stars?* (interviews, books, observations, and travel)

Writing

QUICK ASSESS

Do students' recipes:

✓ identify several characteristics of historical fiction?

✓ explain how Lowry blended her sources?

To help students create original "recipes" for Lois Lowry's historical fiction, bring in some cookbooks and read aloud some actual recipes.

READING AND WRITING EXTENSIONS

➤ Ask students to select a period in history that they find particularly interesting. Have them plan a historical fiction novel that is set during that period. As a start, students can make a list of characters, describe the setting, and discuss possible story ideas.

➤ Invite students to read one of the novels in Joan Lowery Nixon's *Orphan Train* saga, a series that explores the adventures of the six Kelly family children after their widowed mother sends them west on the orphan train to find better lives. Set in Missouri and Kansas in the 1850's and 1860's, and inspired by true stories, these novels will help make history come alive for young readers.

Unit Overview

"Challenging Reading" focuses on students' reading and thinking skills. Although most students have all the tools they need to be good readers and thinkers, they don't often know how to use them. This unit develops students' abilities to use prior knowledge, ask questions, and define in context and helps them know when and even why they should apply these skills. Students will become more confident about using these reading strategies whenever they're confronted with reading material that is complex, confusing, or just plain difficult.

Literature Focus

	Lesson	Literature
1.	Using What You Already Know	**Margery Facklam,** from *And Then There Was One* (Nonfiction-Science)
2.	Asking Questions	**Margery Facklam,** from *And Then There Was One* (Nonfiction-Science)
3.	Adjusting Your Speed	**Kim-Hue Phan,** from "A Personal Narrative" (Nonfiction-Social Studies)
4.	Putting Words in Context	**Alice Calaprice,** from *An Owl in the House* (Nonfiction-Science)
5.	Building Blocks of Words	**Robert Gardner,** "Leonardo da Vinci" from *Experimenting with Inventions* (Nonfiction-Science)

Reading Focus

1. Listing what you already know about a topic helps you get ready for reading.
2. Asking questions before and while you are reading gives you a purpose for reading.
3. When you encounter challenges in your reading, try changing pace, rereading, or reading on.
4. To figure out the meaning of a word you don't know, read the word or words around the unknown word.
5. Figure out the meaning of an unfamiliar word by breaking the word into parts and determining what the parts mean.

Writing Focus

1. Create a cartoon strip about dinosaurs.
2. Write several questions about a piece of nonfiction.
3. Design a strategic reading poster for the classroom.
4. Play a game using word context.
5. Examine word roots to help determine meaning.

One Using What You Already Know

Critical Reading

FOCUS

Your prior knowledge influences the way you react to what you read.

BACKGROUND

In this lesson, students explore how using prior knowledge can help them prepare for reading and become more actively engaged with the text. You might explain that knowing something about a subject beforehand can make it much easier to read and understand new material about that subject. As an added advantage, using prior knowledge sometimes allows us to understand new material on a more sophisticated level.

➤ In the case of *And Then There Was One*, students may already have a strong knowledge base about dinosaurs and extinction. Have them think carefully about what they know before completing the "K" ("What I Know") section of the chart. In the next two lessons, they'll complete the "W" ("What I Want to Find Out") and "L" ("What I Learned") sections.

FOR DISCUSSION AND REFLECTION

➤ Why is it important to use prior knowledge when reading? (Knowing something about a subject beforehand makes it easier to understand new information.)

➤ What are some of the ways readers can "activate" their prior knowledge? (They can use a K-W-L Chart, freewrite, or engage in discussion.)

➤ Ask students to think about where they have learned about dinosaurs. (Responses may include science classes, books, movies—such as *Jurassic Park*—or even funny television shows—such as *Dinosaurs* or *The Flintstones*.)

Writing

QUICK ASSESS

Do students' cartoon strips:

✔ show creativity and a sense of humor?

✔ include facts about dinosaurs?

Students are asked to draw on their prior knowledge in order to create a cartoon strip about dinosaurs. Remind them that creativity—not artistic ability—is what counts.

READING AND WRITING EXTENSIONS

➤ As an extension, have students complete another K-W-L Chart, this time on a subject of their choice. Invite them to be as creative as they like in their choice of subjects. Students will need to locate resources on their topic in order to fill out the "L" ("What I Learned") section of their charts.

➤ Another way to activate prior knowledge is to freewrite. Ask students to freewrite about a topic from one of their textbooks for three minutes. Have them offer as much information as they can think of.

TWO Asking Questions

Critical Reading

FOCUS
Active readers ask questions about what they read.

BACKGROUND
Think of how often young children ask questions. Questioning is their way of attempting to make sense of the world around them. As we grew older, however, we seem to ask fewer questions and make more assumptions. But questioning remains an extremely important part of the learning process. Questions lead us into new territory, causing us to reflect, respond, and ultimately, to deepen our understanding.

➤ As readers, our questions about what we read can help us uncover the underlying meaning of a selection. This is true for fiction, nonfiction, and poetry. So what sorts of questions should readers ask? All questions are valuable, of course, though some questions are more thought-provoking than others. Open-ended questions invite discussion, debate, and reflection. Help students get in the habit of asking these kinds of questions about the literature they read. After they've finished a reading, students can use their open-ended questions in a discussion of the text.

FOR DISCUSSION AND REFLECTION
➤ What kinds of questions should you ask about a text? (Ask factual questions to determine the facts of the selection. Ask interpretive questions to help uncover the underlying meaning of a selection. Ask evaluative questions to understand how you feel about what you've read.)

➤ At what point during a reading should you ask your questions? (Ask questions before, during, and after reading a text.)

➤ Which of your questions about dinosaurs does Facklam's passage answer? (Responses will vary, but you should push students to cite specific details.)

Writing

QUICK ASSESS
Do students' responses:
✓ list 3-4 additional questions?
✓ show a thoughtful reading of the excerpt?

As students complete the "W" and "L" columns of their charts, encourage them to think about what information surprised them. Have them work with a partner and generate several more questions.

READING AND WRITING EXTENSIONS
➤ Play a few rounds of "Twenty Questions" with students. Remind students that the most thoughtful questions are the ones that elicit the most thoughtful responses.

➤ Invite students to look through their textbooks for other nonfiction selections. Have them complete a K-W-L Chart for the selection they find that interests them most. Ask them to pay special attention to the "W" column.

Three Adjusting Your Speed

Critical Reading

FOCUS

Challenging reading demands a variety of reading stategies.

BACKGROUND

Lesson Three offers students some practical strategies that can make it easier for them to cope with difficult selections.

➤ Change the pace of their reading: If they are reading a particularly difficult piece, students can slow themselves down and think carefully about one sentence at a time. Or they can accelerate the pace of their reading to the point that they are skimming. After a quick skim (or preview) of a page or paragraph, they can do a more careful reading of the material.

➤ Reread: Even the most gifted readers return to some selections for a second or third reading, especially if the selection is difficult or confusing.

➤ Ask questions: Each time a reader stops reading and makes a note of a question, he or she digs one level deeper toward the underlying meaning of the selection. Ask enough questions about a text, and eventually readers will begin discovering some answers.

FOR DISCUSSION AND REFLECTION

➤ How did adjusting the speed of your reading help with comprehension of "A Personal Narrative"? (Answers will vary, but students should point to particular places where they slowed down.)

➤ When is it important to reread? (Answers may include because a piece is particularly difficult or confusing and also for enjoyment.)

➤ What questions did you ask as you read Kim-Hue Phan's piece? (Responses will vary, but encourage students to try to answer each other's questions.)

Writing

QUICK ASSESS

Do students' posters:

✓ list several reading strategies?

✓ identify situations where the strategies should be applied ?

✓ have visual appeal?

Students are asked to design a strategic reading poster for their classroom. Suggest that they use colored markers, pictures, and humor to add appeal to their posters.

READING AND WRITING EXTENSIONS

➤ Discuss with students what they know about the Vietnam War in general and the fall of Saigon. If they seem to need additional information, ask them to research the war in the library and then report to the class on what they find.

➤ Have students write a paragraph about the reading strategies that work best for them. What do they normally do when confronted with a difficult selection?

Four Putting Words in Context

Critical Reading

FOCUS

One way to figure out challenging words is to look at the context—the other words around an unknown word.

BACKGROUND

Using context clues takes some practice. Most students either haven't had enough practice or haven't learned the techniques needed to define a word in context.

➤ Remind students that the quickest way to define a word in context is to look at the words or phrases surrounding the unknown word. Surrounding words can explain or define a word, give an antonym or synonym for the word, or offer an example that clarifies the meaning.

➤ Most words can be defined in context, though occasionally readers might have to resort to using a dictionary. One disadvantage to using a dictionary is that it can be time-consuming. Another disadvantage is that a dictionary is not always available when you need it.

FOR DISCUSSION AND REFLECTION

➤ How do you define a word in context? (Try to define a word using clues from surrounding words and phrases.)

➤ Why should you try to define in context before consulting a dictionary? (Defining a word in context can be faster and easier.)

➤ What context clues does Alice Calaprice provide for unfamiliar words? (Responses will vary.)

Writing

QUICK ASSESS

Do students' responses:

✔ create at least two nonsense words?

✔ give a definition for each word?

✔ include sentences that provide context clues to the words' meanings?

Students are asked to play a game using context clues to figure out the meaning of unfamiliar words. They make up two nonsense words, put them in a sentence, and then see if a partner can define the words in context.

READING AND WRITING EXTENSIONS

➤ Alice Calaprice begins with, "A few years ago I did something that I probably shouldn't have done, but to my mind I didn't have much of a choice, really." Ask students to reflect on this sentence and then write a paragraph or two explaining the ways in which they connect this sentence to their own lives.

➤ Ask students to imagine what they think happens to the owlet once Calaprice brings it inside. Does it survive? Have students write a continuation of Calaprice's story. If they like, they can put their continuations in the form of a journal entry.

Five Building Blocks of Words

Critical Reading

FOCUS

When you encounter a long word, try to separate the word into parts.

BACKGROUND

Another way students can improve their speaking, reading, and writing vocabulary is to learn how to slice unfamiliar words into small pieces. Before they can do this, however, students need to understand the uses of prefixes, suffixes, and root words. You might suggest that they spend a little time each day memorizing a new word part and definition.

➤ Students can take their knowledge of word parts and apply them to other subjects, of course. For example, they'll probably encounter these word parts in math, science, or health class:

word part	meaning
centi-	hundred
deci-	ten
milli-	thousand
micro-	million
tera-	trillion
cardio-	heart
gastro-	stomach
osteo-	bone
dent-	tooth
ped-	foot
derm-	skin

FOR DISCUSSION AND REFLECTION

➤ What unfamiliar words does Robert Gardner use? (Answers will vary.)

➤ Ask students to think about why some writers are easier to read than others. Did they find Gardner's piece hard? (Opinions will vary, but help students understand that they may give up too quickly on a writer who uses many unfamiliar words.)

Writing

QUICK ASSESS

Do students' charts:

✓ list a number of unfamiliar words?

✓ show an ability to break words into familiar parts?

✓ demonstrate how to use context and word structure to arrive at meaning?

After circling unfamiliar words in Gardner's writing, students use their knowledge of word parts to figure out word meanings.

READING AND WRITING EXTENSIONS

➤ Have students try out the reading strategies from this unit with challenging reading from their other classes. Have them share specific successes or failures with the class.

➤ Ask students to write about a person whose vocabulary, in speech or writing, they admire—a family member, a friend, a celebrity. How do their words reflect their personalities?

Unit Overview

In this unit, students will discover that they can still read actively and critically when reading for information. The five lessons in "Active Reading: Social Studies" about ancient Egypt lead students through a series of exercises involving previewing, highlighting, summarizing, and using graphics. Students can then take these techniques and apply them to a variety of content areas and genres.

Literature Focus

Lesson	Literature
1. Coming Attractions	from *World: Adventures in Time and Place* (Nonfiction)
2. It's What's Important That Counts	from *World: Adventures in Time and Place* (Nonfiction)
3. Keeping Track	**Elsa Marston,** from *The Ancient Egyptians* (Nonfiction)
4. To Sum Up	**Anne Steel,** from *Egyptian Pyramids* (Nonfiction)
5. Graphs, Maps, and More	**Anne Steel,** from *Egyptian Pyramids* (Nonfiction)

Reading Focus

1. Preview a chapter of a textbook to get an idea of what the chapter is about and how it is organized.
2. Highlighting helps you identify and remember the most important information.
3. Taking notes as you read is another way to help you organize and remember important ideas.
4. Summarizing helps you understand and remember what you read.
5. Graphic sources can help you "see" what you're reading.

Writing Focus

1. Create and write directions for a previewing game to use with a chapter from a social studies textbook.
2. Explain the value of highlighting.
3. Write a magazine article using notes from reading.
4. Design an illustrated trading card about pyramids.
5. Create a graphic about one of the social studies selections in this unit.

One Coming Attractions

Critical Reading

FOCUS

A preview of a textbook chapter can tell you what to expect without revealing everything that's in the chapter.

BACKGROUND

Previewing is a helpful study skill for students no matter what the subject area. Students can preview whether they are assigned a long chapter or even a few pages from a textbook. Explain to students that it's easy to get lost in a textbook, mostly because there is so much information on every page. There are charts, graphs, different types of text, art, diagrams, tables, and so on. Although the graphics in textbooks are helpful, they can make a page seem intimidating.

➤ When students take a moment beforehand to examine the headings, subheadings, and art, they feel more oriented when they actually begin reading the page. Previewing can help them organize their thoughts and their notes.

➤ You might also remind students that previewing can help sharpen their ability to make predictions as they read.

FOR DISCUSSION AND REFLECTION

➤ How is previewing different from reading? (When you preview, you look only at the headings, art, charts.)

➤ In what ways can previewing help with comprehension? (Previewing can help you plan your reading, make predictions, and formulate questions, all of which make the text more accessible.)

➤ How easy was it to preview this passage? (Answers will vary but encourage students to refer to particular parts.)

Writing

QUICK ASSESS

Do students' games:

✓ focus on the rules of previewing?

✓ include directions easy enough for a young child to understand?

Students are asked to create a previewing game for younger students. As a prewriting activity, they'll make a web that shows what they expect to find out when they read the chapter on ancient Egypt.

READING AND WRITING EXTENSIONS

➤ As a further extension, ask students to create the game board and pieces for the previewing game they made. Before they begin, have students carefully review the chapter from their social studies book.

➤ Ask students to use the previewing strategies on a chapter from a school textbook in another subject area. When they've finished previewing, they should create a web similar to the one on page 133 of their *Daybooks*.

TWO It's What's Important That Counts

Critical Reading

FOCUS

When you highlight a selection, underline or circle the information that you feel is most important.

BACKGROUND

In this lesson, students will gain practice in highlighting a selection. Remind them to note everything that they think is interesting, important, and confusing or puzzling.

➤ Highlighting is a particularly important reading technique because it helps readers focus on key aspects of the text. You might want to remind students, however, about the pitfalls of too much highlighting. It won't do the student any good to have almost every word and sentence on the page either underlined or circled. Show students an example of a page or two that you have highlighted.

FOR DISCUSSION AND REFLECTION

➤ Why is highlighting an important technique for reading a textbook? (It helps you keep track of the information that is most important.)

➤ What is involved in highlighting? (Highlighting involves noting anything that is interesting, important, confusing, or puzzling.)

➤ What highlighting techniques might you use if you can't write in your book? (Answers will vary. Students might suggest taking notes on a separate page.)

Writing

QUICK ASSESS

Do students' responses:

✔ explain whether highlighting helps their understanding?

✔ cite specific examples?

After students read the chapter about the Nile and make an information display for a museum exhibit on ancient Egypt, have them reflect on whether highlighting helped them understand what they read. Have them explain their views by referring to specific pages.

READING AND WRITING EXTENSIONS

➤ Ask students to review what they've read about ancient Egypt and then create an illustrated map of the Nile River valley. Have them label important regions, bodies of water, and so on. Later, they might want to visit the library in order to find more information for their maps. Display the maps in the classroom.

➤ Ask students to bring in pictures of Egypt—of ancient landmarks, of the Nile, of current leaders, and so on. Have students use them to make a collage for classroom display.

Three Keeping Track

Critical Reading

FOCUS

Notes are usually a little more detailed than highlighting. Rather than just writing down the main ideas, you also write down details about them.

BACKGROUND

Note taking is an important skill because it helps listeners remember what they've heard and readers remember what they've read. Encourage students to take notes when they read fiction as well as nonfiction.

➤ Remind students to avoid taking notes in complete sentences. Trying to write full sentences will slow them down and make the process much more difficult than it needs to be. As often as possible, students should avoid word-for-word note taking and instead focus on paraphrasing what they hear or read.

➤ Another important aspect of taking notes is figuring out what to do with the notes once they are made. Encourage students to review their notes often—every night, if possible. They'll also want to organize their notes somehow, perhaps with an informal outline or some other organizational tool.

FOR DISCUSSION AND REFLECTION

➤ Discuss students' previous experience with taking notes. Encourage stories of both successes and failures.

➤ Why should you take notes on what you read? (Notes help you remember what you've read.)

➤ What kinds of notes should you take? (Note anything that seems important or that you might want to return to later.)

Writing

QUICK ASSESS

Do students' magazine articles:

✓ include important information?

✓ have a title?

✓ use an engaging style?

Students are asked to write a short magazine article about the Nile. As a prewriting activity, they should review the notes they made while reading and then organize the information into a sequence map. Remind students to create a title and an opening that will interest the magazine's readers.

READING AND WRITING EXTENSIONS

➤ Have students write another magazine article on the Nile, though this time for a children's magazine. Explain that they'll need to consider carefully how they can present the information about ancient Egypt in a simple, engaging way that would appeal to young children.

➤ Have students stop and reflect on what they've learned about ancient Egypt so far. What surprised them? What did they already know? Ask them to write a paragraph or two explaining their reactions to the information in this unit.

Four **To Sum Up**

C r i t i c a l   R e a d i n g

FOCUS

Summarizing can help you remember the important parts of a selection.

BACKGROUND

Remind students that summarizing helps them to think critically about what they've read. Advise students that summaries should be brief and should focus only on the main ideas of a selection. Highlighting and taking notes are both useful ways of preparing a summary.

➤ If students need additional practice summarizing, you might have them write brief plot summaries of a story they have read. (Most readers find it easier to summarize literature than nonfiction.)

➤ To help students fully appreciate Steel's writing, show them pictures of several Egyptian pyramids.

FOR DISCUSSION AND REFLECTION

➤ Explain how you summarize. (You briefly restate material in your own words.)

➤ Why is summarizing an important skill? (It helps you understand and remember the most important information.)

➤ What's the difference between summarizing and quoting? (Quoting is word-for-word; summarizing is restating only the main ideas in your own words.)

W r i t i n g

QUICK ASSESS

Do students' cards:

✔ include some key facts?

✔ have a sketch?

✔ show creativity?

Students are asked to summarize the article and then use their summaries to create a pyramids "trading card." Encourage them to use markers or colored pencils to make the cards more visually appealing.

READING AND WRITING EXTENSIONS

➤ Invite the class to plan an "Ancient Egypt" Web site for the Internet. Working in small groups, students could brainstorm the art, text, or links that might make for an interesting and informative resource.

➤ Ask students to draw a set of illustrations to accompany Anne Steel's article on pyramids. Under each illustration students should write a brief but informative caption that summarizes a few key facts.

Five Graphs, Maps, and More

Critical Reading

FOCUS

Social studies materials use many different types of graphic sources, from maps and charts to diagrams and pie graphs.

BACKGROUND

This lesson tries to explain to students how a good graphic can make complex information easy to understand. You might also want to discuss the various types of graphics found in a social studies text:

- line graph: shows how things change over time

- pie graph: shows proportions and how each proportion or part relates to the whole

- bar graph: uses bars to show quantity or compare subjects being examined

- table: organizes words and numbers so that you can see how they are related

- diagram: shows how something is constructed

FOR DISCUSSION AND REFLECTION

➤ What kinds of graphics would you expect to see in a social studies text? What about a science or math text? (Answers will vary. Students might suggest various graphs, tables, charts, diagrams, and maps.)

➤ Why do authors include graphics? (Answers should include to help readers understand the material and to encourage critical thinking about the information.)

➤ Which graphics do you find easy to understand? Which do you consider most difficult? (Answers will vary. Encourage students to explain their opinions.)

Writing

QUICK ASSESS

Do students' graphics:

✓ help the reader?

✓ convey accurate information?

✓ reflect an imaginative approach to the material?

Students are asked to create a graphic to go with a piece of writing from "Active Reading: Social Studies." Review the previous selections together as they begin to choose possibilities.

READING AND WRITING EXTENSIONS

➤ Have the class work together to build a three-dimensional pyramid out of heavy cardboard or another sturdy material. Ask them to label each part of the pyramid and include with their creation a brief summary of how and why pyramids were originally built. Invite other classes to see the finished product.

➤ Ask students to research some aspect of modern-day Egypt and then report to the class. How has Egypt changed? In what ways has it remained the same? Suggest that they create a graphic to present the information to the class.

EXPOSITORY WRITING

Unit Overview

This unit is designed to help students be better readers of expository nonfiction: newspaper or magazine articles, essays, and textbooks. It is crucial that students have at their fingertips a set of skills that will help them be more critical and effective readers of nonfiction, including finding the main idea, analyzing details, understanding time sequence and cause and effect, and making inferences.

Literature Focus

	Lesson	**Literature**
1.	Finding the Main Idea	**Spencer Christian,** from *Can It Really Rain Frogs?* (Nonfiction-Science)
2.	Dealing with Details	
3.	Searching for Sequence	**Richard Wormser,** from *The Titanic* (Nonfiction-Social Studies)
4.	Considering Cause and Effect	**Richard Wormser,** from *The Titanic* (Nonfiction-Social Studies)
5.	Investigating and Inferring	**Phillip Hoose,** from *It's Our World, Too!* (Nonfiction)

Reading Focus

1. Recognizing the main idea of a piece helps you understand what the piece is all about.
2. Writers use details to support the main idea and to make their writing more interesting.
3. Understanding sequence helps you keep track of information.
4. Recognizing cause and effect relationships helps you connect events and ideas.
5. Inferences help you "read between the lines."

Writing Focus

1. Create a story board or comic strip that explores the author's main idea.
2. Plan an expository article on a familiar subject by outlining the main idea and supporting details.
3. Write a report that describes the sequence of events leading up to the *Titanic* wreck.
4. Write a report on what caused the *Titanic* disaster.
5. Use inferences to write a continuation of an article.

One Finding the Main Idea

Critical Reading

FOCUS

Active readers know that finding the main idea is crucial to understanding what they read.

BACKGROUND

By the time they are in middle school, most students will be fairly adept at finding the main idea, although some may struggle a bit when asked to articulate the writer's central focus.

➤ Before students begin working on Lesson One, you might post this equation on the board:

(subject) + (what the author has to say about the subject) = main idea.

Students can use the equation to help them find the main idea of the Spencer Christian article:

(weather) + (raining frogs; rains of blood and milk, and so on.) = weather can be fun and surprising

➤ Once they've found the main idea, have them explain what leads them to believe that this is the focus Christian intended. Remind them that sometimes a main idea is not expressed directly.

FOR DISCUSSION AND REFLECTION

➤ How do you find the main idea? (Readers should begin by finding the subject. What the author has to say about the subject is the main idea.)

➤ Why is it important to understand the author's main idea? (Understanding the main idea means understanding the meaning the author has for the reader.)

Writing

QUICK ASSESS

Do students' story boards or comic strips:

✓ focus on Christian's main idea?

✓ utilize their notes from reading?

✓ demonstrate careful thought and preparation?

Students are asked to draw a story board or comic strip that reflects Spencer Christian's main idea. They should use the notes they made while reading the text to help them develop ideas for their art.

READING AND WRITING EXTENSIONS

➤ Ask students to write another page or two to be included in Christian's book. Students should write about "wacky weather," just as Christian does. Encourage students to try to keep the tone of their writing consistent with the tone of *Can It Really Rain Frogs?*

➤ Ask students to find and read another book, newspaper article, or magazine article about weather. Have them present a summary of the selection's main idea. Invite them to explain why they did or did not enjoy what they read.

Two Dealing with Details

Critical Reading

FOCUS

Details are "helpers" for the main idea in the same way that your fingers are "helpers" for your hand.

BACKGROUND

In expository writing, details serve two important purposes: they support the main idea, and they add interest to the writing. Before they begin this lesson, you might ask students to think about how the details of a piece of writing can make the writing more lively and memorable. How can details help make a subject "come alive"? Encourage them to cite particular examples if they can.

➢ In some instances, an author will provide details by telling an anecdote or two (as Christian does) in order to make the writing more lively. In other cases, the writer will offer readers a "you-are-there" description of a place or an event.

FOR DISCUSSION AND REFLECTION

➢ What would Christian's article be like without details? (The article would be dull, difficult to read, and less effective, because the details are needed to support Christian's main idea.)

➢ What makes Spencer Christian's details effective? (Answers will vary. Students might note that Christian includes two eyewitness accounts, which make the article interesting and memorable.)

Writing

QUICK ASSESS

Do students' writings:

✔ focus on a subject they know well?

✔ clearly state a main idea?

✔ list several supporting details?

Students are asked to prepare an expository piece on a familiar subject by mapping out the main idea and supporting details. Before they select their topics, have the class brainstorm some possibilities on the board.

READING AND WRITING EXTENSIONS

➢ What's the wildest and wackiest weather students have ever seen? Ask them to explain what they saw in a paragraph. Remind them to include plenty of description and detail so that readers can envision the scene.

➢ Newspaper and magazine writers generally use the formula of one main idea and several supporting details. Ask students to choose articles at random from different newspapers. Have them work together in small groups to identify the main idea and supporting detail of each piece.

Three Searching for Sequence

Critical Reading

FOCUS

Some expository writers use time-order sequence as a way of organizing their writing:

"Then at 11:39 P.M., Fleet suddenly spied an object which at first seemed small but rapidly increased in size."

BACKGROUND

To help students understand sequence, consider relating the skill to a concrete example. For instance, ask students to watch as you tie a pair of shoes, clean the blackboard, or pantomime a multi-step task. When you've finished, ask for volunteers to retell your actions in the correct order.

➤ Many of your students will be familiar with the *Titanic* disaster, of course. However, they might not be familiar with the specific chain of events that led up to the boat striking the iceberg. Explain to students that each event or occurrence in the chain somehow impacts the outcome.

➤ After they've finished reading the Wormser article once, you might ask students to activate their prior knowledge about the *Titanic* and have them put together a more detailed analysis of the sequence of events.

FOR DISCUSSION AND REFLECTION

➤ What is time-order sequence? (explaining a sequence of events in the order in which they occurred)

➤ Why is it important to keep track of the sequence of events or occurrences when reading expository nonfiction? (In many cases, you can find clues about outcomes by examining the sequence or pattern of events.)

➤ Were you surprised by any of the information Wormser presents? (Responses will vary. Invite students to make comparisons between James Cameron's 1997 movie blockbuster, *The Titanic*, and Wormser's piece.)

Writing

QUICK ASSESS

Do students' reports:

✓ demonstrate understanding of the sequence of events in the article?

✓ address the question of whether the disaster could have been avoided?

Students are asked to write an "official" report that summarizes the events leading up to the *Titanic* disaster. Have them share their diagrams of the events in sequential order before they begin the report.

READING AND WRITING EXTENSIONS

➤ Have students write about a frightening event that they witnessed or heard about. The event might be a storm, a fire, an accident, or any other occurrence that set them on edge for at least a moment or two. Ask them to describe what happened using time-order sequence.

➤ Invite students to locate information on another disaster—the San Francisco earthquake, for example, or the volcanic eruption near Pompeii. Then have them diagram the sequence of events leading up to the disaster, as they did for this lesson.

Four Considering Cause and Effect

Critical Reading

FOCUS

Recognizing causal relationships helps readers organize information:

"The rock-hard base of the iceberg had scraped the *Titanic*'s hull below the waterline, gashing some holes in her side and loosening the steel plates that held her together."

BACKGROUND

As you begin this lesson, explain to students that in a cause-and-effect relationship, a cause triggers an event which, in turn, can become the cause of another event, and so on. For example, the absence of shipboard binoculars causes the lookouts' inability to see the icebergs, and that leads to the ship being damaged and the loss of more than 2,000 lives.

➤ Notice that although Wormser provides ample description of how the *Titanic* looks and sounds as she sinks (the effect), he spends more time discussing the various causes behind the wreck. In the excerpts that students read for Lesson Three and Lesson Four, Wormser drops hints about some of the causes of the wreck.

FOR DISCUSSION AND REFLECTION

➤ According to Wormser, what are some of the causes of the *Titanic* disaster? (Answers will vary. Students may suggest these causes: poor look-out procedures, low bulkhead compartments, not enough lifeboats.)

➤ Would you say the disaster was primarily a result of mechanical failure or human error? Why? (Answers will vary. Ask students to support what they say with evidence from the selection. They might also use prior knowledge as support.)

Writing

QUICK ASSESS

Do students' reports:

✓ show they understand the relationship between cause and effect?

✓ identify several specific causes?

Students are asked to state the causes of the *Titanic* disaster and then include them in the report they began in Lesson Three.

READING AND WRITING EXTENSIONS

➤ Ask students to compare Wormser's account of the *Titanic* disaster to a documentary, Hollywood movie, or television version of the same event. Have them discuss which felt more "real" to them—what they read or what they watched.

➤ Discuss with students how many literary works feature a character who undergoes a change as a result of a crisis. Have students think of a character who changes and write about the causes behind the change.

Five Investigating and Inferring

Critical Reading

FOCUS

When you make inferences, you "read between the lines."

BACKGROUND

This lesson invites students to explore an important part of reading: making inferences about the underlying meaning of the selection. In "Essentials of Reading," students examined ways to make inferences while reading fiction. In this lesson, they will consider the many different kinds of inferences they can make while reading nonfiction.

➤ Although this passage about Sarah Rosen reads like fiction, it is actually a nonfiction account of a young girl's efforts to fight discrimination in her school. Angered by her teacher's decision to exclude girls from participating in a school event, Sarah decides to stage a protest.

➤ As they read the article, students should make inferences about the students and teachers involved in the dispute. They might infer, for example, that Dr. Calvin is tough but fair and that Mr. Star has a hard time relating to all of the students in his class.

FOR DISCUSSION AND REFLECTION

➤ What kind of person is Sarah Rosen? What kind of person is Dr. Calvin? (Answers will vary. Ask students to offer specific characteristics and then support what they say with evidence from the selection.)

➤ Why do you think Sarah is so upset by the "no girls, no minorities" rule? (Answers will vary. Students might suggest that Sarah is upset because she hates injustice of any kind or because she herself is determined to participate in the event.)

➤ Why do you think Mr. Star refuses to change the rule? (Answers will vary, but students need to support their inferences.)

Writing

QUICK ASSESS

Do students' continuations:

✔ focus on the girls' demonstration?

✔ utilize the inferences about Sarah, her teacher, and the principal?

✔ model Hoose's tone and style?

Students are asked to write a continuation of the Sarah Rosen article. As they focus on what will happen at the girls' demonstration, remind students to try to imitate Phillip Hoose's style and tone.

READING AND WRITING EXTENSIONS

➤ Invite students to read their continuations aloud and then have the class vote on the versions they like best. Divide the class into groups and ask each group to act out one continuation of Sarah Rosen's story.

➤ Have students read the rest of *It's Our World, Too!* (or another book or magazine that tells real stories about kids). Ask them to write a book or magazine review and then share it with the class.

Unit Overview

This unit invites students to explore style and structure—the meat and potatoes of an author's craft. Students are encouraged to notice word choice, sensory language, sentence style and length, and stanza divisions as they read and respond to several poems and an excerpt from a novel.

Literature Focus

	Lesson	Literature
1.	Words That Work	**Lucille Clifton,** "let there be new flowering" (Poetry)
2.	Getting the Picture	**May Swenson,** "Waking from a Nap on the Beach" (Poetry)
3.	A Thumbprint of Words	**Jerry Spinelli,** from *Maniac Magee* (Fiction)
4.	Setting the Pace	
5.	Structure and Meaning	**Edna St. Vincent Millay,** "The Courage That My Mother Had" (Poetry)

Reading Focus

1. Authors choose words carefully to create specific feelings in readers.
2. Writers use sensory images to spark readers' imaginations and make literature memorable.
3. Every author has a unique way of using language. This is called the author's "style."
4. Sentence structure helps to set the pace of a story.
5. Poets use structure to show what ideas or images are important in a poem.

Writing Focus

1. Describe and then explain your feelings about the wishes expressed in a poem.
2. Create an image poem filled with sensory description.
3. Rewrite a passage in a different style.
4. Rewrite a passage from a novel in order to slow down the pace.
5. Identify and analyze a poem's message by drawing images to represent each stanza.

One Words That Work

Critical Reading

FOCUS

Authors often choose words that carry unspoken messages:

"let there be new flowering / in the fields…"

BACKGROUND

Because most poems have relatively few words (as opposed to a story or an article), word choice is extremely important to poets. Explain to students that poets deliberately choose words that will have a strong emotional impact on the reader. You may want to review connotations with the class.

➤ Lucille Clifton uses a series of strong, emotionally evocative words in her poem, "let there be new flowering." Point out that this poem is an example of a "hope" or "wish" poem, although Clifton never comes right out and says what she is wishing for. Instead, she relies on her language to give readers clues about what she wants.

➤ Students will probably infer that Clifton's wish is for peace—a new beginning or new flowering. She conveys her wish by offering words that conjure images of tranquillity ("mellow" and "tender") and images of springtime—the green fields, the men working the land. In sharp contrast to Clifton's "peace" words are the words she uses that suggest images of violence and destruction: "wrested" and "war," for example. These "negative" words help Clifton explain exactly why she wishes for peace.

FOR DISCUSSION AND REFLECTION

➤ Describe the mood (the feeling a piece of literature arouses in a reader) of Clifton's poem. (Responses will vary, but students should appreciate how Clifton's choice of words contributes to the mood.)

➤ How does Clifton's lack of punctuation affect your reading of the poem? (Answers will vary.)

Writing

QUICK ASSESS

Do students' notes:

✔ describe the speaker's wishes?

✔ explain their feelings about the wishes in the poem?

Have students share their drawings or descriptions of the speaker's wishes before they explain their own feelings about the wishes.

READING AND WRITING EXTENSIONS

➤ Invite students to write a poem beginning with Clifton's words "let there be new…" about a person they admire. Have them share their creations with the class.

➤ Invite students to select a story or poem they enjoy very much and pay special attention to the author's choice of words. Have them pick out several words that give them especially positive feelings.

Two Getting the Picture

Critical Reading

FOCUS

Sensory images help you imagine the things the author describes:

"Sounds like big / rashers of bacon frying."

BACKGROUND

Writers use imagery to bring freshness and immediacy to their writing. In poetry, imagery helps the reader experience the same tastes, sights, smells, and sounds that the speaker does.

➤ In Swenson's "Waking from a Nap on the Beach," the reader is both an observer and a participant. Thanks to Swenson's sensory language, we can visualize the scene and "watch" as the sunbather sits up from a nap. We can feel the speaker's confusion in those first moments in the same way that we can "hear" the roar of the surf and "feel" the heat of the sun.

➤ Directly related to the imagery that Swenson offers is the extended metaphor that she builds one line at a time. In each line of the poem, she makes a comparison between the sea and a pan of bacon frying. This comparison helps unify the poem and draws attention to Swenson's message about the strength, magnitude, and power of the sea.

➤ Invite students to consider the rhythm of "Waking from a Nap on the Beach." Notice how the tempo of the poem builds slowly but surely, one beat at a time. Swenson has created a rhythm structure that mimics the slowly gathering strength of a wave in the ocean. This slow build makes the crescendo of the poem (or wave) seem all the more startling and vivid.

FOR DISCUSSION AND REFLECTION

➤ What is imagery? (Imagery is the words or phrases a writer selects to create a certain picture in the reader's mind. Imagery is often based on sensory details.)

➤ Which sensory images in Swenson's poem leave the strongest impression in your mind? Why? (Answers will vary. Students should explain why the image is effective.)

Writing

QUICK ASSESS

Do students' poems:

✔ help readers imagine the sights, sounds, tastes, and smells of the beach?

✔ reflect their own unique view of the topic?

Students are asked to write an image poem. Before they begin, they should share their webs discussing things about the beach that appeal to the five senses.

READING AND WRITING EXTENSIONS

➤ Invite students to use the sensory details in their image poems to create a sketch that captures the feelings they wish to express.

➤ Ask students to create another image poem that is opposite in mood to the one they wrote for this lesson. For example, if they wrote a poem that explores the joys of the beach, have them write a poem about a storm, a lost child, or a broiling sun.

hreeA Thumbprint of Words

Critical Reading

FOCUS

Paying attention to a writer's style helps us understand what he or she is trying to say.

BACKGROUND

An author's style is usually consistent. It remains the same (or close to the same) no matter how many poems, stories, or articles he or she writes. Of course, not every writer's style is remarkable. Some writers use a plain, unadorned style that serves to emphasize their plot and message. Other writers—Jerry Spinelli included—have highly distinctive styles that can strike a strong chord with readers.

➤ In all of his writing, Spinelli uses a reader-friendly, conversational style and tone. His characters speak in short, unfinished sentences that are full of slang and colloquialisms. A large part of his appeal stems from the fact that his narrators sound like real kids who are entertaining and easy to relate to.

FOR DISCUSSION AND REFLECTION

➤ What is style? (Style is how the author uses words, phrases, and sentences to form his or her ideas. Style is also thought of as the qualities and characteristics that distinguish one writer's work from the work of others.)

➤ How would you describe Spinelli's style? (Spinelli uses short sentences and sentence fragments. His style is quick and conversational with vivid sensory description and many slang words.)

➤ What similes do you find effective? Why? (Responses will vary, but may include McNab "was like a shark," he "was breathing like a picadored bull," or McNab's cap was "spinning like a flying saucer.")

Writing

QUICK ASSESS

Do students' rewrites:

✔ present a contrast to Spinelli's passage?

✔ replace lines and words appropiately?

✔ show the impact style has on writing?

Students are asked to rewrite a passage from *Maniac Magee* and then comment on how their rewrite compares with the piece as a whole. As a prewriting activity, students will decide if Spinelli's style makes it easy or hard to "get into" the story.

READING AND WRITING EXTENSIONS

➤ Jerry Spinelli's style is distinctive. Invite students to read more of Spinelli's writing and then compare and contrast the selection they read to the excerpt from *Maniac Magee*.

➤ Ask students to continue the story by writing a paragraph about what happens next. Encourage them to use sentence fragments, slang words, and vivid sensory imagery to imitate Jerry Spinelli's style.

Four Setting the Pace

Critical Reading

FOCUS

Short sentences can speed the action of a story:

"McNab was loving it . . . He was like a shark. He had the blood lust."

BACKGROUND

Many students have a difficult time analyzing the underlying structure of a story. They can't conceive of a piece of writing being organized in any way other than the way it is organized. You might begin this lesson by explaining to students that writers have a choice when it comes to structuring their work. They can break paragraphs often or hardly at all. They can build to a climax quickly or slowly. They can change the length of their sentences to speed up or slow down the pace. It's up to them to decide how to tell the story.

➤ In *Maniac Magee*, Spinelli uses a structure that allows him to maintain high levels of tension in the narrative. He tells the story about the baseball game in play-by-play form, thereby building reader expectations and interest. Students should note that Spinelli's story starts out slowly, with minimal tension. The tension begins to increase as Maniac steps up to the plate. With each ball that McNab throws, the tension goes up one more notch.

FOR DISCUSSION AND REFLECTION

➤ What is structure? (Structure is the form or organization an author uses for her or his writing.)

➤ Why is sentence length important? (It can help set the pace of a story. In addition, structure can enhance a reader's enjoyment and help shed light on the author's message.)

➤ Where is the high point of tension in the story? (Responses will vary but might include when McNab throws the ball at Maniac's head.)

Writing

QUICK ASSESS

Do students' rewrites:

✓ use longer sentences?

✓ add detailed description?

✓ lower the tension level?

Students are asked to restructure one passage from *Maniac Magee*. Before they begin, have them share their charts of the highs and lows of the tension in the story.

READING AND WRITING EXTENSIONS

➤ Have students describe a tense moment they remember vividly—participating in a sports championship, giving a speech, awaiting an important phone call, or watching a horror movie. They should use short sentences and sentence fragments to create a fast pace.

➤ Invite students to page through their *Daybooks* to find an example of a passage they think is fast-paced and one that they feel is slow-paced. Have them write a paragraph that compares and contrasts the structures of the two passages.

Five Structure and Meaning

Critical Reading

FOCUS

A poem's structure offers clues to its meaning.

BACKGROUND

This unit is meant to deepen students' understanding of poetic structure and sharpen their ability to read and respond to poetry. You might start out by encouraging students to look carefully at each of Millay's three stanzas. Millay has created a kind of sandwich poem, with the two stanzas on the outside exploring her theme of courage, and the one stanza in the middle making a comment on tangible versus intangible gifts.

➤ Although the speaker is clearly saddened by her mother's death, this is not a poem of mourning. In many ways, in fact, it is a poem of celebration. The speaker rejoices in her memories of her mother's physical beauty (represented by the golden brooch) and the beauty of her spirit (her courage and generosity).

➤ Notice also that the final line of the poem is a "bad rhyme" (*grave* and *have* are slightly off in sound, although their spellings might lead you to believe that they do rhyme). Millay's unusual rhyme draws special attention to the final words of the poem and the speaker's true reason for reflecting on her mother's courage.

FOR DISCUSSION AND REFLECTION

➤ What is the poem's structure? (The poem has three stanzas of verse; each stanza has four lines.)

➤ Describe Millay's style. (Her poem has an irregular rhyme scheme, although she does use at least one set of rhyming lines in each stanza. She uses one simile and a great deal of repetition, consonance, and assonance.)

Writing

QUICK ASSESS

Do students' responses:

✓ create a strong image for each stanza of the poem?

✓ show understanding of Millay's meaning?

Before students describe Millay's meaning in their own words, as a prewriting activity, they should try to visualize the imagery of each stanza and share their sketches in small groups.

READING AND WRITING EXTENSIONS

➤ Invite students to write a poem about a person they admire, using Millay's three-stanza structure as a model.

➤ Invite students to describe the structure of a poem they like. Have them comment on the length of the lines, the stanza breaks, and the poet's message.

Unit Overview

"Active Reading: Poetry" will provide students with tools that will help them become critical readers of poetry. Many students find poetry intimidating, either because they can't figure out what the poet is trying to say or because they can't understand the structure of the verse. This unit helps students with both points of confusion—structure and meaning—and at the same time proves to them that poetry can be lively and fun and pleasurable to read. Poems by Margaret Walker, Gary Soto, Mary TallMountain, Ogden Nash, and Maya Angelou are featured.

Literature Focus

	Lesson	Literature
1.	The Poem on the Page	**Margaret Walker,** "Lineage" (Poetry)
2.	Tuning In	**Gary Soto,** "Finding a Lucky Number" (Poetry)
3.	Beyond Words	**Mary TallMountain,** "There Is No Word for Goodbye" (Poetry)
4.	Word Music	**Ogden Nash,** "Adventures of Isabel" (Poetry)
5.	The Beat Goes On	**Maya Angelou,** "Life Doesn't Frighten Me" (Poetry)

Reading Focus

1. You can begin to understand a poem by looking at its layout on the page.
2. Poets use sensory images to help convey their messages and create strong impressions.
3. Exploring figures of speech deepens your insights into a poem.
4. Noticing rhymes and echoes helps you hear the music of a poem.
5. Rhythms in poetry help to communicate feelings to readers.

Writing Focus

1. Interpret a line from a poem.
2. Sketch an image from a poem and then add notes that explain the visual image.
3. Write a short poem that uses imagery.
4. Add rhyming lines to a poem by Ogden Nash.
5. After groups perform a poem, emphasizing its sound and rhythms, compare the effects of the different versions.

One The Poem on the Page

Critical Reading

FOCUS

The look of a poem can give clues to its meaning.

BACKGROUND

Explain to students that it's always a good idea to give a poem a quick once-over before sitting down to read each verse carefully. Consider how it looks on the page. Encourage students to notice the layout, stanza divisions, and length of the poems they read. Have them pay attention to capitalization, punctuation, and anything else that catches their eye. Many times the arrangement of the poem will provide clues about the poem's underlying meaning.

➤ In "Lineage," Margaret Walker uses straight lines, linear spacing, and two stanzas of six lines apiece (two sestets). She uses an iambic (an unstressed syllable followed by a stressed syllable) pentameter (five metric feet) pattern, thereby imitating the rhythm of spoken English. Because her rhythm is familiar, it is accessible to readers. This makes her final line—"Why am I not as they?"—feel immediate and to the point. This question, Walker seems to say, is a question we all need to be asking ourselves.

FOR DISCUSSION AND REFLECTION

➤ What aspects of a poem should you consider when asked to analyze the layout? (Answers should include placement of the poem on the page, word spacing in individual lines, and how the poem has been divided into stanzas.)

➤ What poets seem to do a lot of experimenting with the structure and layout of their poetry? (Answers will vary. Students may suggest E. E. Cummings, Shel Silverstein, or any other poet with a distinctive style.)

Writing

QUICK ASSESS

Do students' responses:

✓ focus on the meaning of the last line of "Lineage"?

✓ reflect a careful reading of the poem?

Before students explain Walker's closing question, suggest that they try to characterize the speaker and how she feels about herself.

READING AND WRITING EXTENSIONS

➤ Invite students to write a "lineage" poem of their own that features one or more of their family members. Encourage them to use Walker's "Lineage" as a model for their style.

➤ Read E. E. Cummings's poem "Mouse) Won" to students, and then show them how it looks on the page. Discuss together Cummings's unusual choices about capitalization, punctuation, line breaks, and stanza divisions.

Two Tuning In

Critical Reading

FOCUS

Poets use sensory details to create strong images:

"Up an alley, as I rolled chocolate / In my mouth and looked around / with my face."

BACKGROUND

When an author uses sensory language in his or her writing, it is much easier for readers to visualize what the author is describing. In Lesson Two, "Tuning In," students explore how sensory language can help create vivid images in the reader's mind as they examine a poem by Gary Soto. Students may be familiar with Soto as a poet, short-story writer, and novelist. Much of his work (particularly *Local News*, a collection of short stories set in a neighborhood outside of San Diego) focuses on his own Mexican American background.

➤ "Finding a Lucky Number" is filled with the kind of imagery that helps readers taste, hear, see, and touch almost everything the poet describes. From the very first line, Soto invites the reader to take a walk with the speaker and experience everything that the speaker experiences. For example, we'll "taste" the chocolate, "see" the blue sky, "smell" the spilled garbage, and "hear" the clicking dominoes.

➤ Because we walk side-by-side with the speaker and experience all the same things that the speaker experiences, we can't help but feel the same sense of confusion ("And I, not knowing what to do, looked in") that the speaker feels when the old man in the park opens his mouth wide. We are caught off guard and surprised (just as the speaker is) by the revelation that lucky number twelve is "lucky" because it is the exact number of yellow teeth left in this man's mouth.

FOR DISCUSSION AND REFLECTION

➤ What is your favorite example of sensory language in Soto's poem? (Answers will vary, but have students explain the image they choose.)

➤ Why do poets like to use sensory language in their writing? (Sensory language makes writing fresh and vivid. Authors use this type of imagery as a way of appealing to the reader's imagination.)

Writing

QUICK ASSESS

Do students' sketches:

✓ represent one image?

✓ include notes explaining the image?

Insist that students read the poem several times before they make a sketch of one image from the poem, and then make notes that explain the sketch.

READING AND WRITING EXTENSIONS

➤ Have students write a personal note to Soto. Ask them to begin their notes with this sentence: "Your poem made me feel _____."

➤ Divide the class into three small groups. Then ask each group to work together to turn Soto's poem into a short story, fairy tale, or fable. When they've finished, have them share their work with the whole class.

Three Beyond Words

Critical Reading

FOCUS

Active readers know how to explore figures of speech:

"When does your mouth / say goodbye to your heart?"

BACKGROUND

In "Beyond Words," students will learn about figurative language and then apply what they've learned to a poem by Mary TallMountain. Explain that the most common types of figurative language include simile, metaphor, and personification.

➤ An example of a simile, a comparison of two unlike things in which a comparison word (like or as) is used is "She touched me light / as a bluebell." An example of a metaphor, a comparison of two unlike things in which no comparison word is used, is "Sokoya, I said, looking through / the net of wrinkles into / wise black pools / of her eyes." An example of personification, a literary device in which the author speaks of or describes an animal, object, or idea as if it were a person is "When does your mouth / say goodbye to your heart?"

➤ As further background for this lesson, you might review the "Author's Craft" unit with students. Simile, metaphor, and personification are explored in some detail there.

FOR DISCUSSION AND REFLECTION

➤ What examples of figurative language do you find in TallMountain's poem? (Students might note these examples of figurative language: two metaphors in stanza one, personification in stanza four, and a simile in stanza six.)

➤ What is the effect of this figurative language? (Answers will vary. Help students to see that TallMountain's figurative language makes the poem fresh, vivid, and unique.)

Writing

QUICK ASSESS

Do students' poems:

✔ evoke one of TallMountain's figures of speech?

✔ use imagery and details?

Students are asked to select an image from TallMountain's poem and then develop it in a poem of their own.

READING AND WRITING EXTENSIONS

➤ Invite students to write a paragraph in which they use one simile and one metaphor to describe a favorite place or object.

➤ Have the class work together to come up with a list of stale, overused metaphors and similes — such as "quiet as a mouse," "cold as ice," or "life is a bowl of cherries."

Four Word Music

Critical Reading

FOCUS

Critical readers pay attention to a poem's sounds as well as its meaning:

"Isabel, Isabel didn't worry, / Isabel didn't scream or scurry."

BACKGROUND

As students begin this lesson, "Word Music," remind them that not all poems have to rhyme; however, many students will prefer rhymed verse to unrhymed verse. This may be because rhymed poetry is often easier to read, and—for some—reminiscent of rhymes or songs they learned as children. Rhyme does more than just enhance enjoyment of a poem, however. It also serves to unify the work and reinforce meaning.

➤ Ogden Nash uses the most common type of rhyme—called end rhyme—in "Adventures of Isabel." To help students understand Nash's rhyme, chart the first stanza's rhyme scheme on the board, beginning with:

Isabel met an enormous bear,	a
Isabel, Isabel didn't care;	a
The bear was hungry, the bear was ravenous,	b
The bear's big mouth was cruel and cavernous.	b

➤ Nash also uses assonance and consonance echoes in his poem: "Ho, ho, Isabel! the old witch crowed, / I'll turn you into an ugly toad!" (assonance, /o/ sound) and "She showed no rage and she showed no rancor" (consonance: /sh/ and /r/ sounds). This sound repetition helps Nash create a playful, childlike mood that matches exactly the poem's playful, childlike message.

FOR DISCUSSION AND REFLECTION

➤ What are some examples of sound devices? (Students might suggest rhyme, rhythm, alliteration, assonance, consonance, onomatopoeia, and repetition.)

➤ Why do poets use sound devices? (Sound devices unify a work, enhance enjoyment, and reinforce meaning.)

➤ How do the rhymes of Nash's poem emphasize its humor? (Responses will vary, but ask students to cite specific lines and examples.)

Writing

QUICK ASSESS

Do students' lines:

✔ rhyme?

✔ maintain the playful tone of the poem?

Students are asked to create one or more rhymes of their own and then add them to "Adventures of Isabel."

READING AND WRITING EXTENSIONS

➤ Ask students to review what they know about another sound device—onomatopoeia or alliteration, for example—and then see if Nash uses that device in "Adventures of Isabel." They might explain their discoveries in a paragraph or two.

➤ Ask students to examine the lyrics of a popular song and note how many examples of sound devices the lyrics contain. Invite them to share their findings with the class.

Five The Beat Goes On

Critical Reading

FOCUS

The rhythms of a poem affect readers' enjoyment and understanding:

"Panthers in the park / Strangers in the dark / No, they don't frighten me at all."

BACKGROUND

In "The Beat Goes On," students are asked to think about how rhythm can affect their enjoyment and understanding of a poem. To further their understanding of rhythm, explain to students that rhythm is the ordered or free occurrences of sound in poetry. If the rhythm is ordered or regular, it is called *meter*. If it is irregular, it is called *free verse*.

➤ Maya Angelou's "Life Doesn't Frighten Me" has a regular, albeit varied, rhythm. Students should notice that Angelou's poem is very much like a song you might hear on the radio, in part because she repeats the line "Life doesn't frighten me at all" in much the same way that a songwriter repeats his or her refrain. Also, point out that the rhythm, or tempo, of the poem picks up in the middle after a slow, smooth beginning and that the poem ends on a "resonant" note—two additional characteristics of musical composition.

➤ Students should take note of the ways Angelou uses repetition to reinforce her message and unify the poem. In addition to the repeated phrase, "Life doesn't frighten me at all," Angelou repeats language patterns within stanzas ("Bad dogs barking loud / Big ghosts in a cloud"; "Panthers in the park / Strangers in the dark") and from stanza to stanza.

FOR DISCUSSION AND REFLECTION

➤ What is the difference between rhyme and rhythm? (Rhyme is the similarity or likeness of the end sounds between two words; rhythm is the ordered or free occurrences of sound in poetry. To put it another way, rhyme is the pattern, and rhythm is the beat. Meter is an organized or regular rhythm.)

➤ What kind of mood is created by the rhythm and rhyme in Maya Angelou's poem? (Responses will vary. Have students support their ideas with examples from the poem and encourage them to comment on one another's views.)

Writing

QUICK ASSESS

Do students' presentations show:

✓ an understanding of rhythm?

✓ creativity?

✓ planning and practice?

Urge students to be creative in planning their group performances of Angelou's poem. If possible, videotape their presentations and view them together before asking students to write about the different versions.

READING AND WRITING EXTENSIONS

➤ Explain to students that much of Angelou's poetry has a musical feel to it. Invite them to read and analyze more of her verse. How would they describe her poetic style? Have students write a "Poet's Profile" that they can then present to the class.

➤ Ask students to choose a song by their favorite singer or group and write out the lyrics as a poem, with line and stanza breaks. Then ask them to analyze the rhythm and note any changes in tempo.

PERSUASIVE WRITING

U n i t   O v e r v i e w

Although students are exposed to a variety of persuasive messages—such as those in speeches, reviews, editorials, and advertisements—they are not always certain how to evaluate the value or effectiveness of those messages. In this unit, students will examine some of the elements of persuasive writing: connotations, bias, facts and opinions, and tone.

L i t e r a t u r e   F o c u s

	Lesson	Literature
1.	The Emotional Impact of Words	**Nicolette Toussaint,** "Hearing the Sweetest Songs" (Nonfiction)
2.	Where Is the Writer Coming From?	**Nicolette Toussaint,** "Hearing the Sweetest Songs" (Nonfiction)
3.	Taking Sides	**Steven Levy,** "The Myth of the Computer" (Nonfiction)
4.	Separating Fact from Opinion	
5.	Tone	**Robert Fulghum,** from *All I Really Need to Know I Learned in Kindergarten* (Nonfiction)

R e a d i n g   F o c u s

1. Writers use connotations to encourage their readers to respond emotionally to a topic.
2. Recognizing a writer's viewpoint can help you evaluate the writer's ideas.
3. Biased writing tries to persuade the reader to see an issue from one particular side.
4. Writers use facts to support their viewpoints.
5. Persuasive writers use tone to encourage their readers to feel a certain way about a topic.

W r i t i n g   F o c u s

1. Create two menus, using positive and negative connotations.
2. Write a note to an author, explaining whether reading her article changed your viewpoint.
3. Analyze an author's bias and compare it to your own bias on the same topic.
4. Make notes for a debate by listing facts and opinions that support your viewpoint.
5. Evaluate an author's tone.

One The Emotional Impact of Words

Critical Reading

FOCUS

Active readers are aware of the emotional impact of certain words:

"We're all just temporarily abled, and every one of us, if we live long enough, will become disabled in some way."

BACKGROUND

One way to help students understand how a word's connotations can affect the writing is to have them practice identifying word connotations and denotations. Try writing several sentences on the board:

1. This clock is *old*. 3. The woman was *self-confident*. 5. He is *timid*.

2. This clock is an *antique*. 4. The woman was *arrogant*. 6. He is *shy*.

Ask students to decide whether the connotation of each *underlined* word is favorable or unfavorable and then explain why.

➤ Nicolette Toussaint's piece works particularly well for a lesson on connotation and denotation because it is mainly a discussion of how a word like *disabled* can color everything a person sees, thinks, and does: "Once someone is labeled 'deaf,' 'crippled,' 'mute,' or 'aged,' that's too often all they are." According to Toussaint, words like these carry such strong connotations that it's often impossible to see the person behind the word.

FOR DISCUSSION AND REFLECTION

➤ What's the difference between connotation and denotation? (A denotation is a word's dictionary meaning; a connotation is the emotional meaning of the word in addition to its dictionary meaning.)

➤ How can a writer use connotation as a persuasive technique? (If you use words with negative connotations, your readers will be inclined to share your negative perspective on a topic or issue. The same is true for using words with favorable connotations.)

➤ How did Toussaint feel when she started to wear a hearing aid? (Responses should stress that it was not easy for her. Toussaint felt anxious and on edge.)

Writing

QUICK ASSESS

Do students' menus:

✔ show an understanding of connotation and denotation?

✔ show creativity?

Students are asked to write two menus for a school lunch: one using denotation and one using connotation. Urge them to add humor as they create names for their dishes.

READING AND WRITING EXTENSIONS

➤ Ask students to come up with a list of five adjectives that describe themselves and then identify words with the same denotative meaning but very different connotations. For example, if they describe themselves as "thrifty," they might also be "cheap." If they are "naive," they might also be "trusting."

➤ Invite students to write a letter to Toussaint explaining what they think is the emotional impact of her piece. What did Toussaint's writing mean to them?

Two Where Is the Writer Coming From?

Critical Reading

FOCUS

Persuasive writers want their readers to share their viewpoints.

BACKGROUND

In this lesson, students focus on the importance of a persuasive writer's purpose and perspective. Remind students that every person's viewpoint on an idea, issue, or topic is unique. Our perspectives are ours and ours alone, even if we share some opinions in common with other people.

➤ Suggest that students think of perspective as a suitcase we carry around with us all our lives. The things that go into our suitcases—our sex, our appearance, our religion, our experiences, our family and friends, and so on—are the things that help form our perspectives. Our perspective, in turn, colors everything we see and do and write.

➤ To help them understand Toussaint's perspective in "Hearing the Sweetest Songs," you might ask students to brainstorm a character profile for Toussaint. What are some of her likes and dislikes? What's important to her? What's her personality like? If they take the time to think about who Toussaint really is, students will have an easier time understanding her message.

FOR DISCUSSION AND REFLECTION

➤ What would you say is Toussaint's purpose for writing? (Answers will vary, but they should include that she writes to inform and persuade.)

➤ What do you think Toussaint's message is? (Answers will vary. A possible response is that she wants us to look beyond a person's disabilities so that we can try to understand who the person really is.)

➤ What is your reaction to her message? (Answers will vary. Students need to support their ideas with their own experiences or the experiences of others.)

Writing

QUICK ASSESS

Do students' notes:

✓ explain their perspectives?

✓ analyze the effect the article had on their perspectives?

Students are asked to write Toussaint a note explaining their perspective on the topic and noting whether the piece affected their viewpoints. As a prewriting activity, they create a web that explores Toussaint's perspective in "Hearing the Sweetest Songs."

READING AND WRITING EXTENSIONS

➤ Invite students to write a journal entry about a time they felt they were judged by how they look instead of by their character. What happened? What was their reaction? Were things resolved? Why or why not?

➤ Toussaint makes an interesting point in her article: "We're all just temporarily abled, and every one of us, if we live long enough, will become disabled in some way." Ask students to react to this opinion. Do they agree? Why or why not?

Three Taking Sides

Critical Reading

FOCUS

All persuasive writing has bias:

"I'm not sure how good computers really are for kids."

BACKGROUND

"Taking Sides" begins by opening students' eyes to the fact that most (if not all) writing has some bias. It's almost impossible for a writer to be completely unbiased or neutral about a topic. Of course, some types of writing are more biased than other types. For example, a newspaper editorial offers a highly biased view of an issue or topic, while an article in an encyclopedia will likely be much more neutral. To extend their learning on this topic, you might ask students to bring in a recent newspaper and then examine bias in various features, the stock market reports, an editorial cartoon, and so on.

➤ Steven Levy's "The Myth of the Computer" provides students with a clear example of slanted or biased writing. Although his own career "is intimately entwined with the digital revolution," Levy makes it clear that he doesn't think of computers as the best educational tools around. He supports his claim by writing about his own child, who was computer literate at a young age—but probably no smarter or better off as a result.

➤ Help students notice that Levy uses an inductive arrangement for his argument. He builds his argument slowly, one detail at a time ("I was 30 years old before I touched a computer"), until he feels ready to make his main point ("The superstar of education is still the book"). By building up to his main point, Levy puts special emphasis on his assertion.

FOR DISCUSSION AND REFLECTION

➤ What is bias? (Often bias is strongly favoring someone or something. Bias can also be negative.)

➤ Where do you frequently see some examples of biased writing? (Answers may include in an editorial or magazine column, a letter to the editor, a book review, a movie review, or an advertisement. Almost all writing, in fact, has some degree of bias.)

Writing

QUICK ASSESS

Do students' responses:

✔ correctly identify elements of Levy's bias?

✔ explain their own views on the same topic?

✔ identify their personal bias?

Students are asked to examine Levy's bias and then analyze their own positions on this topic. Before they begin, initiate a discussion of their first experiences with computers: how old they were when they first used one, what software they liked, and so on.

READING AND WRITING EXTENSIONS

➤ Have students listen to a news reporter's account of a local event or sports contest and see if they can detect bias. Have them summarize their findings for the class.

➤ Invite students to try a little biased writing of their own. Ask them to argue for or against Levy's idea that there should be a computer at every student's desk. Remind them to offer support for their viewpoints.

Four Separating Fact from Opinion

Critical Reading

FOCUS

Persuasive writing usually contains both facts and opinions.

BACKGROUND

In this lesson, students are asked to consider the difference between fact and opinion and the role the two play in persuasive writing. Explain to students that every argument begins with an opinion. In persuasive writing, the writer's opinion is called the claim, or assertion. The writer uses facts to support the assertion.

➤ One of the reasons Steven Levy's "The Myth of the Computer" is effective is that he offers his audience an engaging (and persuasive) mix of fact and opinion. He establishes an opinion-fact-opinion rhythm early on and never deviates from it. This makes for an argument that has a strong and well-supported feel. Have students analyze the following as an example: "I'm not sure how good computers really are for kids. My own progeny, born in 1990, was perched before a screen well before he turned 2, with more familiarity with a wired mouse than the squeaky variety. He took for granted what 20 years ago would have been considered outrageous: unlimited access to a computing machine with more power than the room-filling-multi-million-dollar military behemoths of the past."

FOR DISCUSSION AND REFLECTION

➤ How does Levy feel about children using computers? (Answers will vary. Students might note that he is in favor of some computer use, but he still believes that books are the best educational tools.)

➤ Which facts and opinions in "The Myth of the Computer" do you find most convincing? (Accept responses that students can support.)

➤ What facts might Levy add to make his piece more persuasive? (Suggestions will vary.)

Writing

QUICK ASSESS

Do students' notes:

✓ clearly state a viewpoint?

✓ use both facts and opinions to support the position?

Students are asked to explain Levy's view of computers, evaluate his argument, and then make notes for a debate about computer use. Remind them to draw on a mix of opinions and facts as support.

READING AND WRITING EXTENSIONS

➤ Ask students to write a short (three- or four-paragraph) position paper explaining their feelings about the use of computers in schools. Ask them to consider the role computers should play in the classroom and whether there should be limitations on computer use for schoolwork.

➤ Have students write a review of a movie or television series that most of their peers know well. Have them include several opinions about it. Then ask another group to read the review and brainstorm facts that could be used to support the opinions.

Five Tone

Critical Reading

FOCUS

A writer's choice of tone influences our perception of his or her viewpoint.

BACKGROUND

As students begin this unit, it would be wise to spend some time discussing tone with them. Explain to students that tone is the author's attitude toward his or her subject or audience. Suggest that the first place to look for clues about tone is in the author's word choice. Is the language formal? strong? emotional? flowery? In each case, the language will set the tone for the writing.

➤ Robert Fulghum's tone in *All I Really Need to Know I Learned in Kindergarten* is rhythmic and soothing. He maintains a slow, gentle pace throughout. He uses simple words and short paragraphs. This makes his writing easy to read and understand.

➤ Like many writers, Fulghum matches his tone to his message. He wants to persuade readers to be kind and gentle, so he uses a kind and gentle tone. He wants readers to recall their kindergarten experiences with affection, so he imitates the smooth, nonthreatening tone of the kindergarten teacher. Using tone in this manner is a highly effective persuasive technique. It's almost as if the reader finds himself or herself being carried gently along, lulled into agreement.

FOR DISCUSSION AND REFLECTION

➤ What is tone? (Tone is the author's attitude toward his or her subject or audience.)

➤ What is the relationship between word choice and tone in a piece of writing? (A possible response is that an author's word choice can establish or enhance the tone of a piece of writing.)

➤ Describe Fulghum's tone. (Answers may include kind, gentle, warm, friendly, and sincere.)

Writing

QUICK ASSESS

Do students' responses:

✓ describe Fulghum's tone?

✓ explain how his tone affects his message?

Have students share the images they drew reflecting the tone of the piece. Then they'll write about whether Fulghum's tone helps persuade his readers. If students have difficulty, suggest that they try imagining how Fulghum could have conveyed his message with different words and style.

READING AND WRITING EXTENSIONS

➤ Have students write about a time when someone spoke to them in a tone of voice they didn't like and/or they felt was inappropriate.

➤ Invite students to recall and reflect on what they learned in kindergarten. Then have them make a list and compare it to Fulghum's list.

Unit Overview

In this unit, students will explore the life and stories of Gary Paulsen. Students will examine Paulsen's style, discover how he bases characters on people he knows, and explore how his writings involve a variety of challenges. To give them a sense of Paulsen—the writer and the person—students will read several passages from three different novels and an excerpt from his autobiography, *Woodsong*.

Literature Focus

	Lesson	Literature
1.	An Author's Style	from *The River* (Fiction)
2.	Real-Life Characters	from *Dancing Carl* (Fiction)
3.	Personal Challenges	from *Dancing Carl* (Fiction)
4.	Challenges in Nature	from *Dogsong* (Fiction)
5.	Autobiographical Writing	from *Woodsong* (Nonfiction)

Reading Focus

1. A writer's style can affect the impressions readers get as they read.
2. Basing a character on a real person helps writers create characters that seem vivid and real.
3. When you read about a character confronting a challenge, try to figure out how and why the experience changes the character.
4. Reading about characters confronting challenges in nature gives us a glimpse of how people act and think when tested by extreme conditions.
5. Writers share events from their own lives not only to tell what happened, but also to tell what makes those events important.

Writing Focus

1. Continue Paulsen's story, imitating his style.
2. Complete a character sketch chart for someone you know.
3. Use a chart to explore changes in a character.
4. Rank the challenges a character faces and explain your rankings.
5. Write notes for your own autobiography.

One An Author's Style

Critical Reading

FOCUS

Apart of Paulsen's appeal is his conversational writing style:

"He couldn't be. He couldn't be...dead. Not Derek."

BACKGROUND

Gary Paulsen, who has won numerous awards for his writing, is popular with young readers for two reasons: one, because his writing style is simple, straightforward, and reader-friendly; and two, because his plots are exciting, engaging, and believable.

➤ Paulsen's style, which is as fast-paced as his plots, is characterized by short sentences and rapid-fire paragraphing. He rarely pauses for detailed description, though he clearly establishes time and place. Paulsen tends to use a great deal of dialogue in his stories. This makes for highly involving reading.

➤ Paulsen is known for his suspenseful plots. Paulsen's story lines are often quite involved, though they are never excessively complicated or difficult to follow. Even the most reluctant readers are easily drawn into a Paulsen narrative.

FOR DISCUSSION AND REFLECTION

➤ What is an author's style? (Style is how the author uses words, phrases, and sentences to form his or her ideas. Style is also thought of as the qualities and characteristics that distinguish one writer's work from the work of others.)

➤ How would you describe Paulsen's style? (Paulsen's style is characterized by short, rapid-fire sentences and paragraphs.)

➤ Does a "staccato" style make for easy or difficult reading? Why? (Encourage students to explain their varying responses.)

Writing

QUICK ASSESS

Do students' paragraphs:

✓ continue the story in a believable way?

✓ imitate Paulsen's style?

✓ communicate tension and excitement in their writing?

Students are asked to add to the excerpt, trying to imitate Paulsen's style.

READING AND WRITING EXTENSIONS

➤ Ask students to predict what they think will happen to Derek and Brian. Will both of the men survive? Have students write a paragraph in which they explain their predictions.

➤ Have students imagine they are Gary Paulsen and have been asked to give a speech on the importance of a simple writing style. Ask students to write the introduction for that speech.

TWO Real-Life Characters

Critical Reading

FOCUS
Sometimes authors base characters on real people.

BACKGROUND

Like most writers, Gary Paulsen tends to write what he knows. Many of his characters are people he met at one point or another, and many of the situations he describes happened to him or to someone he knows.

➤ In *Dancing Carl*, Paulsen introduces one of his most memorable characters—Carl, a kind-hearted, though emotionally disturbed war veteran. Paulsen presents Carl's problems through the eyes of a young boy. The boy—Marsh—is an honest, trustworthy narrator who clearly wants to tell the reader everything, no matter how difficult or disturbing.

➤ In this excerpt, we see a Carl who is both menacing ("his eyes look hot") and kindly ("he moved into the middle and he took a little girl by the hand and shouldered people out of the way…"). He is determined to help the downtrodden—the children who cry because there is no room for them—even if it means intimidating everyone around him.

FOR DISCUSSION AND REFLECTION

➤ Why do you think Carl wants to help the young children? (Students might note that because Carl is somewhat childlike himself, he can empathize with the smaller children's needs, or that Carl is a kind man who knows what it's like to feel confused or ignored.)

➤ What can you infer about Marsh's attitude toward Carl? (Answers will vary. Marsh seems puzzled by Carl's actions and both intimidated and fascinated by Carl's strangeness.)

Writing

QUICK ASSESS
Do students' charts:

✔ lists descriptive traits and experiences?

✔ demonstrate understanding of how to fictionalize characters based on real people?

Students are asked to write about someone they know who might make an interesting character in a story. They will fill out a chart that can help them "fictionalize" the person they have in mind.

READING AND WRITING EXTENSIONS

➤ Invite students to draw a portrait of the Carl they visualized when reading. Under the portrait, have them write a two-sentence explanation of who Carl is and what he's like.

➤ Ask students to imagine they are Marsh. Have them write a letter from Marsh to the town council in which he either complains about Carl or tells the council what a great job Carl is doing at the rink.

Three Personal Challenges

Critical Reading

FOCUS

Active readers identify the key incidents that shape a character's personality and attitudes.

BACKGROUND

In "Personal Challenges," students will be asked to read another excerpt from *Dancing Carl*. Here again they'll see two different sides to Carl's personality. In many ways, Carl is a kind, caring man who is happy to have befriended Marsh, Willy, and the other children ("He smiled when we came in…"). In other ways, he is deeply disturbed, a man who behaves "as if something inside had ripped and torn loose and left him broken."

➤ When the boys bring the B-17 model to the warming house, something in Carl snaps. He begins to recall a terrifying experience he had during the war. Instead of merely telling about the experiences, however, he actually "becomes" the B-17 bomber.

➤ Although Carl is clearly unstable and perhaps even menacing, the reader still feels sympathy toward him. This is because Paulsen describes him with compassion and helps the reader to "see" (through Carl's vivid reenactment of his war experience) why Carl is the way he is.

FOR DISCUSSION AND REFLECTION

➤ What is internal conflict? (a personal or emotional challenge that a character faces)

➤ What is Carl's internal conflict? (Answers will vary. Students might suggest that he is torn between memories of a horrible war and his desire to live and function in the here and now.)

➤ Why are the boys so frightened by Carl's response to the model? (Explanations will vary.)

Writing

QUICK ASSESS

Do students' charts:

✓ reflect understanding of how Carl changes?

✓ include several specific character traits?

Students are asked to complete a chart about how Carl's war experiences changed him.

READING AND WRITING EXTENSIONS

➤ Ask students to create the conversation they think that Marsh and Willy might have had as they watched Carl twirl. In keeping with the situation, the conversation between the two boys should be quick, intense, and fearful.

➤ Have students create a diagram that shows what occurs in these two excerpts from *Dancing Carl*. What is the sequence of events? When they've finished, ask students to explain how the outcome would have been different had one of the events not occurred. For example, how would things have been different had Marsh left the model at home?

Four Challenges in Nature

Critical Reading

FOCUS

Some plots pit a character against a challenge in the natural world:

"He'd never felt so alone and for a time fear roared in him."

BACKGROUND

In this lesson, students read an excerpt from *Dogsong*, in which Gary Paulsen presents readers with a riveting account of one man's struggle to survive in the wilderness. In this story and in others, Paulsen explores what is clearly one of his favorite questions: What skills are necessary to win a battle against nature? Paulsen makes us wonder whether wits alone are enough to guarantee survival. Can a hatchet be a key to survival?

➤ This excerpt opens with an exhausted and frightened Russel searching for a place to rest. He worries mostly that the dogs will give out on him, that they'll stop pulling the sled and leave him stranded in the Alaskan wilderness. A big part of Russel's problem, in fact, is that he is unwilling to put complete faith in the dogs. He doesn't trust them explicitly, and they don't trust him explicitly. This inability (or unwillingness) to trust in or cooperate with the natural world is a recurring theme in Paulsen's writing.

➤ In many of Paulsen's stories, it is the unknown problems that cause the most trouble. For example, in *Dogsong*, Russel worries about the dogs, the frigid temperatures, and the food supplies. It never occurs to him to worry about the terrain, and it is the land that ends up posing the most problems for the team.

FOR DISCUSSION AND REFLECTION

➤ What kinds of conflicts are common in literature? (person-against-person, person-against-nature, person-against-self, person-against-society)

➤ What kinds of conflicts does Paulsen present in *Dogsong*? (person-against-nature and person-against-self)

➤ What happens if a story lacks conflict? (The reader is bored and indifferent to the outcome. Conflicts create the dramatic structure that compels a reader to keep turning pages.)

Writing

QUICK ASSESS

Do students' charts:

✓ rank the challenges in order?

✓ explain their rankings?

Students are asked to choose four challenges in nature that Russel encounters and then rank them from 1 to 4. Have students compare their charts with what others have done and explain their decisions.

READING AND WRITING EXTENSIONS

➤ Ask students to read the rest of *Dogsong* and then make a "map" of Russel's journey. Have them note his starting point, where things end, and the challenges he faces along the way.

➤ What can students infer about Russel? Have them use their inferences to write a character sketch of him.

Five Autobiographical Writing

Critical Reading

FOCUS

Paulsen describing his own conflict with nature:

"For not hurting me, for not killing me, I should kill him? I lowered the rifle and ejected the shell and put the gun away. I hope Scarhead is still alive."

BACKGROUND

In this lesson, students read and respond to an excerpt from Gary Paulsen's autobiography, *Woodsong*. What's most interesting about *Woodsong* is that it gives readers an "insider's" glimpse of Paulsen and how similar he is to the characters he invents. Like many of his characters, Paulsen has struggled with some natural-world challenges. Eventually, he comes to the understanding that humans must live cooperatively with the natural world. Many of his characters (especially the characters in his survival stories) come to the same realization.

➤ In this excerpt, Paulsen describes a true-life conflict of person-against-nature (Paulsen vs. Scarhead). For a few rash moments, Paulsen attempts to control (or conquer) nature by shooting the bear. He quickly comes to his senses, though, and decides not to kill him. He acknowledges the supremacy of nature and feels humbled by his dealings with the bear.

FOR DISCUSSION AND REFLECTION

➤ Why do authors often choose to write what they know? (Answers will vary, but they may include that if you draw from your own experiences, your writing may seem more authentic, more realistic.)

➤ What similarities do you see between Paulsen's *Woodsong* and his works of fiction? (Answers will vary. Encourage students to support their responses.)

Writing

QUICK ASSESS

Do students' notes:

✔ describe a challenging experience?

✔ use plenty of details?

✔ reflect on how the experience affected them?

Students are asked to think of a challenging experience they once had and then prepare notes for their own autobiographies. Remind them not only to describe the experience in detail, but to include comments about what they learned from it and how it changed them.

READING AND WRITING EXTENSIONS

➤ Tell students that Paulsen's run-in with the bear caused a bit of a stir in a nearby town. Have them write a news story to reflect this "breaking" news.

➤ Paulsen considers *Woodsong* his finest work. Ask students to write a paragraph explaining why they agree or disagree with his assessment.

Most activities in the *Daybook* ask for open-ended, creative responses. As a result, only selected activities where specific answers are possible are included here. The intent is to help the teacher by clarifying a possible or partial response to the question, not to specify the one complete, true answer. The process of writing in response to literature and interacting with a text is the main goal of the *Daybooks*. Answers are given here only for the convenience of teachers who may want further clarification of specific activities.

PAGE 18: Students' charts will differ. The following is an example:

Taylor's Craft	In *The Gold Cadillac*	In "Author's Note"
Are there "fancy" words? Give examples.	Cadillac, café, uppity, heedful	meticulously, mar, exasperation, concession, admonished, freedom-loving, raucous
Are there words that create a picture? Give examples.	Outright stopped, good-natured, loaded gun, mighty dangerous, lynch, shiver,	rusty, August-like, cool forest trails, kicking testily, gritty red snow, dust billowed in swirling clouds
How does the selection feel? (for example: happy, sad, thoughtful)	The selection feels hesitant, pensive, then scary.	The selection feels personal, warm, and thoughtful.
What words would you use to describe Taylor's writing? (for example: descriptive, lots of dialogue, very detailed)	Her writing is descriptive, and she uses dialogue well to create a picture.	Her writing is reflective and personal.

PAGE 19: Students' index card notes will vary. Following is a general example, without specific text references:

Main Idea: Mildred Taylor is a skilled writer; her craft is especially evident in her use of descriptive words and phrases.

Details: In "Author's Note," *Roll of Thunder, Hear My Cry*, and *The Gold Cadillac*, she uses dialogue and colorful expressions to tell personal stories:

  • in the first, expresses love/respect for her father, a great storyteller, a week after his death

  • in the second, uses vivid descriptions and dialogue to make an ordinary first day of school not so ordinary

  • in the third, uses a situation involving their car to confront the topic of racism

Conclusion: Taylor's upbringing, especially her father, had a large influence on her as a writer. She thoughtfully recalls everyday events and makes them special through her use of colorful words, descriptions, and dialogue.

PAGE 21: Taylor depicts Tom Bee as heroic by his not giving in to the white man's demands, even though he was in severe pain. Students' charts will vary, but might look like the following:

Taylor's Perspective	shows "the Black person as heroic"	shows "a family united in love"	shows "parents, strong and sensitive"
In The Friendship	Yes. Tom Bee is a hero because he stands up for himself.	no family here	no parents here
In The Gold Cadillac	Yes. Her parents are willing to risk getting lynched.	Yes. Her mother supports her father's decision.	Yes. Her mother and father take a firm stand to do what they feel is right.
In Roll of Thunder, Hear My Cry	nothing heroic in excerpt	Yes. Although they seem to be arguing, the siblings share common feelings.	Yes. The older siblings are looking out after the younger ones.
In "Author's Note"	Yes. Taylor sees her father as a hero.	Yes. She and her father have a common respect for family and a love for words.	Yes. Her father was firm and consistent; he taught her many things.

PAGE 23: Students' connection charts will differ, but an example follows:

Connection to Taylor's Life	
The Gold Cadillac	I know that the narrator and her family live in Ohio because the Gold Cadillac has Ohio license plates. Taylor lived in Ohio when she was a child.
Roll of Thunder	Cassie discusses sharecropping in the story. In her "Author's Note," Taylor tells of a family history of slavery and of the days following slavery, which usually consisted of sharecropping.
The Friendship	Tom Bee experiences racism, as did Taylor and her family.

PAGE 24: Students' introductions of Mildred Taylor will vary. Below is an example:

Mildred Taylor is a talented writer who is especially good at describing events from her own life. She is an African-American writer and confronts such topics as racism and slavery in candid ways. Taylor is skilled at using dialogue to get a point across. Her descriptions are sensitive and thought-provoking. Taylor credits her success as a writer to her father, also a master storyteller.

PAGE 28: Students' predictions will vary. A sample prediction might be that Margot causes the sun to appear.

Students should continue the story based on their own previous predictions. Below is a sample prediction.

Margot remembered the sun and added a few more lines to her poem. The sun was like a penny round and shiny. She longed to see it and feel it as she had only five years earlier. The incessant pounding of the rain, though, was all she could feel and think and taste and see and hear and smell. Venus was no good for her.

Completing her poem would do it; Margot knew what it would take for the sun to appear, for the rain to stop. The others didn't believe her. "She is crazy," they said. Margot began to read her finished work aloud. The rain seemed to be slowing down.

PAGE 34: Students' main idea equations should be similar to the following:

Indians	+	people's wrong views of Indians	=	Most people don't understand Indians
(subject)		(what the author says about subject)		(main idea)

The sentence that best expresses the author's main idea is the last sentence of the article: "They just don't understand Indian people." Personal writing and main idea equations will vary.

PAGE 36: Students' Response notes will vary, but they might mark the poem in the following way:

We're sitting at table,	
all of us,	
sighing with the joy	Express feelings
of too much good food	
and Gramps says,	
"When I was a boy . . ."	
and we all snore	Entertain
because we know	Persuade
we've heard it before	
about how he had to	Entertain
patch his shoes and	
chop the wood	
and catch the goose	
and . . .	
But we listen	Teach
(and even the snore is	Entertain
part of it, surely)	
because if we didn't,	Persuade
our hearts	Express feelings
would miss it sorely.	Teach

PAGE 37: Students' attitudes toward the poem will differ. Holman's purpose is to convince readers that even though adults might seem out of touch or boring, they will be missed when they're not around. Don't take people for granted.

Students' responses will vary, but Holman could have achieved her purpose in many ways—for example, by writing an autobiography, a short story, a letter, or an article.

PAGE 40: Students should underline or circle the following sentences and phrases in *The Search for Delicious*:

"There was a time once when the earth was still very young, a time some call the oldest days."

"This was long before there were any people . . . ."

"People came along much later . . . ."

". . . (which nearly always fell down after a while) . . . ."

". . . on the earth in that early time . . . ."

Students should underline or circle the following sentences and phrases in *A Wrinkle in Time*:

"But where am I?"

"They were standing in a sunlit field . . . ." (Students should include this complete sentence; it describes place.)

"Around them everything was golden with light."

"The grasses of the field were a tender new green . . . ." (As above, students should include the complete sentence.)

". . . to face a mountain reaching so high . . . ." (Students should include the rest of the paragraph; it describes place.)

PAGE 41: The reader can visualize the setting in *A Wrinkle in Time* more clearly because the writer uses more adjectives, more descriptive phrases.

PAGE 42: Students' Response notes should include the following:

Danny's father was not a stern, serious man; he smiled with his brilliant blue eyes instead of with his mouth.

His father was not a very educated man; he probably didn't read 20 books in his entire life. However, he was a great storyteller and would make up bedtime stories every evening.

His father was very intent, pale, still, and distant when telling stories.

His father would affectionately hold his son's hand as he told bedtime stories.

PAGE 43: Students' opinions of Danny's father will differ, but most will reflect some of the following characteristics:

Danny's father seemed to be very loving and caring.

He must have felt that his son was important to spend time every night telling his son such wonderful tales.

He was creative and ingenious in coming up with creative stories that continued for many nights.

Danny's father seemed to take his storytelling very seriously.

PAGE 44: Students' word pictures will vary, but some of the words they might use to describe Danny's father include genuine, loving, unselfish, creative, intent, affectionate, smiling, blue-eyed, storyteller, imaginative, sincere

PAGE 48: The first paragraph is the exposition; the remainder of page 48 and pages 49 and 50 are the rising action; the climax starts with the last paragraph on page 50 and continues at the top of page 51; the falling action starts with the first complete paragraph on page 51 and continues until the last paragraph; the resolution is in the last paragraph on page 51.

PAGE 52: Students' plot mountains should be similar to the following:

Exposition: Monk and Glennie are playing baseball beside the firehouse; Scho notices them.

Rising Action: Scho joins them to play ball. He doesn't have his glove, so he gets slow grounders; Scho stops and waits to use Monk or Glennie's glove. He climbs a tree and says he can make the other two do whatever he wants them to do. Monk gets mad and climbs the tree after Scho. Monk threatens to shake the branches Scho is sitting on.

Climax: Scho falls from the tree. He lands on his back with a deep thud. Monk says he honestly didn't touch him; Monk and Glennie ask how he is.

Falling Action: Scho rolls over, smiles slightly. Monk apologizes and Scho says he meant Monk to do it. Monk and Glennie walk away.

Resolution: Scho shouts out in pain and triumph that he wants the other two boys to do whatever they're going to do for the whole rest of their lives.

Students should combine the previous list of events to summarize the story's plot.

PAGE 53: Students' views of the author's intent will vary. Below is an example:

The author most likely wants readers to realize the value of friendship; if friends are considerate enough to invite you to join them, you shouldn't tease, taunt, or irritate them. Otherwise, they will not want you around.

Students' statements of theme will vary, but following is an example:

Treat others as you would wish to be treated and cherish their company and friendship.

PAGES 58: Students' webs should contain the following information:

Utzel: small, miserable-looking, grouchy, looks adoringly at his daughter, poor, lazy, tired

Poverty: heavy, tall, broad, dressed in rags, wore no shoes, had fat puffy feet the size of a man's, spread out in all directions

PAGE 61: Most students will say they are surprised by the changes in the characters b[...] Utzel and Poverty had been poor and lazy for so long; the author does not prepa[...] reader for these sudden changes.

PAGE 62: Students' speeches will vary, but following is an example:

Ladies and gentlemen, thank you for having enough faith in me and for trusting me enough to elect me as warden of the charitable loan society. It means a great deal to me; I am very familiar with the loan society. I turned to the loan society when I was in need. The society loaned me five gulden to buy a pair of shoes for my daughter.

My daughter and I were very poor—so poor, that my daughter did not have shoes. My wife had died of starvation, and my daughter and I were left depressed, tired, and unmotivated. However, I truly love my daughter and had to do something to make her life better. That opportunity came as a result of meeting Mr. Sandler, the shoemaker. I never would have met Mr. Sandler had I not taken out the loan for new shoes.

I learned from Mr. Sandler that the only way to really make it in this world is to work hard for want you need. So, that is what we did. My daughter and I found jobs, and we have never been happier. I am no longer tired all the time, but instead motivated and grateful. I rebuilt my home and have all the furniture and food I need. My daughter's life has changed tremendously: she is healthy, happily married, and, yes, she now has plenty of shoes.

PAGE 65: Students' profiles will differ, depending on which character they find most interesting. Below is an example:

PERSONALITY PROFILE OF: UNCLE HILARY		
Question	**Your Answer**	**How Do You Know?**
How old is the character?	Middle aged	Uncle Hilary is rather set in his ways: he complains about hotels, trains, new languages, and his stomach having to endure strange foods.
Is the character friendly of unfriendly?	Friendly	He is offering to take his young nephew on a vacation. He also jokes around.
Is the character quiet or noisy?	Noisy	Uncle Hilary talks a lot. He might be too noisy: Ned's father is always a little touchy when Uncle Hilary's around.
Is the character smart?	Yes	He speaks well and he is well-traveled. He also knows a lot about other places.
What does the character look like?	Smiles quite a bit; looks exciting	Uncle Hilary smiles at Ned. He looks exciting because Ned thought his uncle looked "like electricity."

PAGE 67: Students' responses will vary, but an example follows:

Kim's thoughts and feelings before planting the beans:

Kim hoped her father's eyes (in his photograph) would notice her. She cried the day after the anniversary of her father's death. She was hesitant about going into the vacant lot to plant the lima beans. She didn't know her father because she was an infant when he died and she had no memories of him. Worse, he never knew her.

Kim's thoughts and feelings while planting the beans:

Kim becomes more confident; she knows her father now sees her in the vacant lot. He will now watch her and be proud of her. He will see her patience and hard work. Kim knows that by planting the seeds, she will show him that she's his daughter. She is certain the seeds will sprout.

Response notes should include the following:

(or) grape sherbet = gelled light

hor) dollop of sherbet = a miracle

e) sherbet is like salt on a melon

taphor) grape sherbet = lavender

etaphor) grandmother = torch of pure refusal

PAGE 77: Students' opinions will vary, but they might respond that the father "bothers" to make the special dessert because only he knows the secret recipe, and the dessert is so enjoyed by the family. He seems to be proud of his accomplishment.

PAGE 79: Students' Response notes should include that the crow is able to steal cheese and anxious to impress the fox; the fox is able to wish and is witty, and scheming.

Students' feelings about the fox will vary, but most will be impressed with his abilities.

PAGE 82: Students' charts will vary, but a few of the many ways Kennedy's poem appeals to the senses include the following:

Smell: sock feet, raisin bread, wet weather

Touch: back flat on carpet, cushion under head, feet on the wallpaper, and balance on high wire

Sight: The entire poem appeals to the sense of sight by using imagery.

Sound: cushion under head, munching bread, making easy whispers, shrill wistle, and phone makes it thunder

Taste: munching raisin bread

PAGE 85: Students' impressions of Mary Hume will vary, but they will generally say that the most predictable ending of the poem would have been for Mary to think that Heaven did not live up to her expectations either.

PAGE 86: The ending has an ironic twist; it is not what the reader expects. Throughout the poem, Mary complains about everything; nothing meets her expectations. Then, when she arrives in Heaven, the reader expects Mary to find Heaven also unsatisfactory. However, a voice from Heaven states that Mary is not so perfect herself.

PAGE 88: The main idea is that public-school students should be required to wear uniforms. The sentence that best states the main idea is: "Schools across the country should follow the example of Long Beach, Calif., which is requiring public-school students to wear uniforms."

PAGE 90: Students' webs should include the following supporting details:

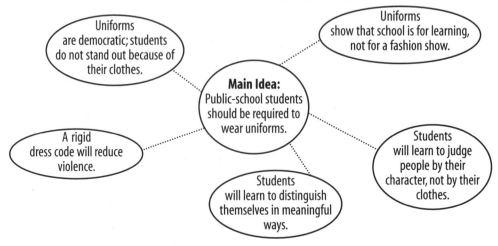

PAGE 93: Velasquez's argument is strengthened by including opposing viewpoints. She shows that robots are important because they can complete difficult tasks, but they still cannot do things that humans can do. In this way, Velasquez demonstrates that she is not personally against robots, that they do have some value, but that the fact is they cannot replace humans.

PAGE 94: Students' charts should include the following information:

Velasquez's viewpoint	Opposing viewpoint
Robots from movies and books—smart, well-behaved, walking—don't really exist.	Robots are smart, well-behaved, and can talk and walk.
Industrial robots do not think or act like humans.	Industrial robots can think and act like humans.
Engineers believe there's little reason to build robots—"mechanical human beings."	Robots are "mechanical human beings."
A baby can do things a robot cannot do.	Robots can perform tasks that people don't enjoy, such as industrial work.
If robots cannot do everything a human can do, then robots will never replace humans.	Robots can do dangerous work that humans shouldn't perform.

PAGE 96: Some of the strategies Halpern uses include giving supporting details and facts to show how single plant species are important to humans and animals, using questioning to probe the possibility that humans are endangering species whose value we have not yet realized, and refuting the opposing viewpoint that the extinction of plants and animals is unimportant.

PAGE 101: Students' responses will differ, but they might feel that Meg and Molly seem to have a normal sibling relationship; they argue and are competitive with each other. Most readers can sympathize with both girls.

PAGE 104: Students' feelings will vary. The following is an example response:

Meg's father is trying to prepare Meg for her sister, Molly's, death. He also seems to be calming his own fears by verbalizing the circumstances. He is preparing the family for a very painful experience by focusing on the fact that Molly just needs their love and support.

PAGE 111: Lowry blends fact and fiction effectively through the use of dialogue and narrative details. Rather than merely list historical facts, she creates interest by developing believable characters and an intriguing plot. Readers then are able to feel connected to the historical facts in a more realistic way.

PAGE 113: Some of Lowry's methods for writing historical fiction include traveling to the area, interviewing people, and making observations about how the people lived; for example, what books they read, what flowers were in bloom, what children played with, what the economic conditions were like, and imagining herself in the situation.

PAGE 124:   Students' charts might look like the following:

Words I Don't Know	Word Meaning
Zoologist	Person who studies animals that live in the wild
Naturalist	Person who studies animals that live in the wild
Fend	To try to get along without help
Captivity	To be locked up; not free
Tempering	Bothering; interfering
Interdependence	Natural balance between plants and animals dependence upon one another
Habitat	Place where plants and animals naturally live
Kinship	Closeness; relationship
Owlet	Baby Owl
Instinctively	Naturally, spontaneously
Docile	Peace loving, calm
Predator	Animal that attacks others in an aggressive manner.

PAGE 128:   Students' charts might look like the following:

Words I Don't Know	Word Meaning
Regarded	Considered
Reveal	To uncover or to make known
Architect	A person who designs buildings and advises in their construction
Botanist	A specialist in botany (the study of plants)
Ecologist	A scientist concerned with the interrelationship of organisms and their environments
Astronomer	A scientist who observes celestial phenomena
Anatomist	A scientist who studies anatomy (the structure of organisms)
Wrath	Anger
Alternately	In the order of taking turns; every other one
Circumvented	Went around
Differential	A differential gear (an arrangement of gears for connecting two shafts or axles in the same line)
Forerunner	One that comes before
Ratchet jack	A jack (mechanical device) that can be moved in steps or degrees
Cam	A rotating or sliding piece in a mechanical linkage; used mostly in transforming rotary motion or vice versa
Reciprocating saw	A saw that can be moved backward and forward alternately
Pipe Borer	A tool that can cut, or bore, through pipes
Pedometer	A device that measures the distance someone has walked
Worm gear	A worm wheel (a toothed wheel gearing)
Dredge	A machine for removing large amounts of earth

Words I Don't Know	Word Meaning
Prefabricated housing	Houses with parts made ahead of time to make assembly easier
Pinions	A gear with a small number of teeth designed to mesh with a larger wheel or rack
Anticipated	Expected

PAGE 133: A sample student web might look like the following:

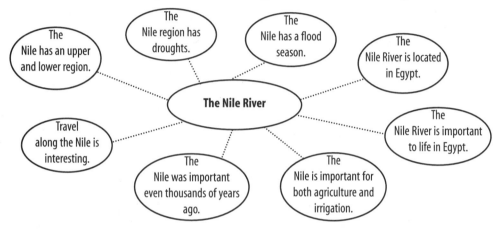

PAGE 134: The main points that students should circle are the following:

"Most Egyptian doctors were priests."

"They learned and practiced medicine in temple schools."

"The world's first medical textbooks were born."

"Some treatments from ancient Egypt are still used today."

PAGE 137: Students' sequence maps will differ, but might look like this:

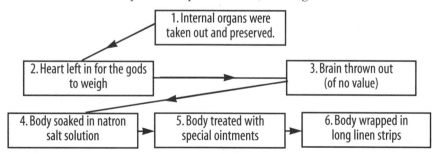

PAGE 146: Students' responses should be similar to the following:

Main Idea: Strange weather occurrences usually have a logical explanation.

Detail: No one has ever observed snakes, frogs, fish, or other animals being carried up into the skies.

Detail: The only logical explanation for these strange rains, however, is that the culprits are tornadoes (columns of air that drop down from storm clouds and twirl at very high speeds) or waterspouts (tornadoes that touch down on water instead of land).

Detail: Large waterspouts have been reported picking up objects as big as a five-ton houseboat, so it makes sense that they could pick up small creatures like fish and frogs.

Detail: These rains were probably colored by small particles of dust or plant pollen that had been blown great distances.

Detail: The Sahara Desert contains areas of reddish iron dust picked up by desert whirlwinds, and in some areas red algae grows so quickly after a storm that it seems as if it fell from the sky.

PAGE 148: Students should underline transitional words such as *by, then, within, as soon as,* and *when it suddenly*.

PAGE 149: Students' diagrams should be similar to the following:

The Titanic approaches an ice field.

↓

Lookout Frederick Fleet realizes the ship is headed for the iceberg. Fleet alerts others on the ship.

↓

In 37 seconds, the Titanic begins its swing away from the iceberg.

↓

First officer William Murdoch gives orders to change the ship's course.

↓

The Titanic is about to hit the iceberg when it suddenly begins to swerve out of the iceberg's way.

↓

The officers think their last-minute efforts have worked.

↓

The ship appears to have only lightly scraped the iceberg.

↓

But passengers and crew below know something worse has happened.

PAGE 151: Students' responses will differ, but they might highlight the following information:

"Four crew members relaxing in a first-class lounge ...."

"Major Arthur Godfrey Peuchen, a Canadian, thought a "heavy wave had hit the ship.""

"Mrs. Walter Stephenson, who had lived through the 1906 San Francisco earthquake, thought the shock felt like an earthquake tremor."

"...as tons of sea water came crashing into the ship. The whole left side of the ship seemed to collapse suddenly."

"...their deck was covered with ice that had fallen from the iceberg."

"The rock-hard base of the iceberg had scraped the Titanic's hull below the waterline, gashing some holes in her side and loosening the steel plates that held her together. Water was rushing into the front of the ship."

"Because the Titanic's bulkheads were not high enough to prevent this from happening, the spill-over would continue from compartment to compartment until the whole ship filled with water and sank."

PAGE 155: Students' Response notes might include the following inferences:

Sarah's teacher discriminates.

Sarah is informed about her rights and the rights of others and cares about being discriminated against.

Sarah is a leader among her classmates.

Dr. Calvin (the black female principal) seems sympathetic to the rights of others.

Mr. Star is stubborn and unwilling to consider other people's rights.

Dr. Calvin is supportive of Sarah's plan to protest against discrimination.

PAGE 157: Students may describe the characters as follows:

Sarah is intelligent, informed, sympathetic, strong-willed, a leader.

Mr. Star is uncaring, biased, chauvinistic, unfair.

Dr. Calvin is sympathetic, understanding, fair, caring, supportive.

PAGE 161: Students' descriptions will differ, but they may include wishes mentioned for flowering fields, mellow fields, tender men, a short, victorious war, and love.

PAGE 165: Students' Response notes should include underlined examples that are labeled F, C, S, and V.

What students select will vary, but they might pick out the following:

"…they just heard it whizzing past their noses. You could see their knees shaking from the stands." V

"His nostrils flared, he was breathing like a picadored bull." C

"Just a punky, runty little kid, no Red Sox or Green Sox uniform." F

"He was back in the box." S

PAGE 169: Students' continuums should be similar to the following:

Maniac steps up to the plate.	McNab throws strikeout #26.	Maniac hits McNab's first pitch.	Maniac swings at the ball like a golfer teeing off.	McNab throws the ball at Maniac's head.

Low tension ←————————————————————————————→ **High tension**

The short, quick lower tension sentences build up to the higher tension, longer sentences.

PAGE 172: The poem's main message is that the speaker needs her mother's courage, rather than the brooch her mother left upon her death. It points to the necessity for personal qualities, rather than material things.

PAGE 174: Students' Response notes and charts will differ. Below are possible responses:

Framing: The poem seems to be framed symmetrically; the top and bottom stanzas look symmetrical. Also, the poem is straight on the left side and ragged along the right.

Word spacing: The lines are straight with regular spacing.

Sections: There are 2 stanzas, each with 6 lines. Shorter lines are at the beginning and end of each stanza. Longer lines are in the middle of each stanza. Students' responses to the poem will vary.

PAGE 178: Some of the figures of speech students should explore are:

"looking through / the net of wrinkles …."

"wise black pools / of her eyes"

"A shade of feeling rippled / the wind-tanned skin."

"watching the river flash."

"We never leave each other. / When does your mouth / say goodbye to your heart?"

"She touched me light / as a bluebell."

PAGE 181:

Examples of rhyming, consonance, and assonance from the first stanza that students should mark include the following:

Rhyming: bear / care; ravenous / cavernous; to / do; meet you / eat you; How / now; worry / scurry; hair up / bear up

Consonance: bear's / big; cruel / cavernous; scream / scurry; hands / hair

Assonance: Isabel / didn't; big / Isabel; cruel / you; ravenous / glad; Isabel / didn't; hands / hair; straightened / ate

PAGE 190:

Students will have different views on what the author has to say. However, most people would view not hearing as a disability. The author generally does not. Instead, Toussaint finds hearing mostly to be a nuisance, except when she would like to be able to hear the alarm clock, doorbell, and potential burglars.

One example of a positive connotation from the story is that the author liked all of the attention she received while having her hearing tested.

The author's negative connotations about not hearing include not being able to hear doorbells, alarm clocks, and potential burglars.

The author's connotations about being hearing impaired are mostly positive.

The author wants readers to realize that, overall, she is not disabled and that people who can hear well are rather disabled by too much noise. Basically, the author finds hearing to be a problem more than not being able to hear.

PAGE 193:

Students' responses will differ. They should, however, realize that the author wants readers to see her and others like her as being slightly disabled, not completely unable. She wants readers to ask if they have questions about her disability, and she wants them to know that she is much more than someone who is "deaf."

PAGE 194:

Below is a sample web:

We are all just temporarily abled; if we live long enough, we'll become disabled in some way.

You will better understand me and my disability if you just come forward and ask questions. I don't mind if you ask.

I don't want to be labeled as "deaf," "crippled," "mute," or "aged."

Toussaint's Perspective
Don't see me as completely different from you or make me feel inferior; I'm much more than a person who can't hear.

Because I can't hear, sometimes waiters think I can't speak either.

I'm a writer, a painter, a slapdash housekeeper, a gardener who grows wondrous roses; my hearing is just part of the whole.

If I tell that I can't hear, I run the risk of being seen as unable rather than disabled.

My disability is an important part of me, something my friends see as part of my character.

I always hated to be seen as inferior, so I never mentioned my disability.

PAGE 197:   Students' continuums will differ, but an example follows:

TOPIC: COMPUTERS

| Extreme Opinion (positive) | Neutral | Extreme Opinion (negative) |

The best way for children to
learn is by computer.

Computers do not help children
learn at all.

The "X" on the continuum marks approximately where the author's bias would fall. Students' responses will vary. Among examples from the article that point out the author's bias are:

"I'm not sure how good computers really are for kids."

"But what did he do with it? At its best, he learned some problem-solving by figuring out the proper order that Putt-Putt the automobile should tackle his chores …."

"There is the worst of it, too. He spends lots of time with silly and sometimes overly aggresive programs."

"And it's great that they provide a means to augment learning, sometimes through startlingly creative programs. But as for computers being a learning panacea, forget it. The superstar of education is still the book."

PAGE 198:   Students should explain that Levy sees the computer mainly as a form of entertainment, not as a means of educating children.

Levy uses opinion to try to persuade readers. He is not very persuasive in that he uses only his son as an example and presents his points in mostly emotional terms. For example, he uses phrases such as "I felt," "I'm not sure," "We all believe," "Silly and sometimes overly aggressive programs," "I was happy that he had learned," "I'm happier to see the kid with a book."

PAGE 200:   Students' Response notes will vary, but they might describe the warm, friendly tone of the excerpt as soft, wise, direct, fuzzy, comfortable, loving.

PAGE 207:   Students might note that Carl seems to be intimidating, understanding, and compassionate to young children, forceful, glaring, effective, tough, a military-type, dominating, unafraid and commanding.

PAGE 208:   Marsh learns that Carl, although tough on the exterior, has a soft spot for little kids, sticks up for the younger kids who can't defend themselves, and is strong and commanding.

PAGE 211:   The narrator, Marsh, sees Carl as breaking down, losing control. Up to this point, Marsh and Willy had no idea that Carl would go so crazy, or break down, over the subject of airplanes. The narrator says, "something inside had ripped and torn loose and left him broken." Carl was broken mentally, not physically.

PAGE 212:   Students' charts might be similar to the following:

Before the War	After the War
Emotionally strong	Emotionally weak
Commanding	Out of control
Confident	Insecure
Sane	Insane
Composed	Broken

PAGE 213:   Some of the sections students may mark include the following:

Russel is in the cold north, out in the open, 150 miles from anything, and his sled dogs are so worn out they can't even eat.

Russel sleeps between the dogs to keep warm.

Russel heads the team north through an area he isn't familiar with.

The sled dogs are losing weight and need to eat meat. So Russel needs to hunt.

In order to hunt, Russel needs to keep warm so that he can keep moving.

While trying to get warm, Russel wears himself out running.

PAGE 214:   The sentence "without the dogs he was nothing" means that without the dogs he may not be able to survive. If the dogs die, he can't walk back on his own; it's too far and too cold. If the dogs die, he could also die.

PAGE 217:   Students' charts will differ, depending on the character they chose. Below is an example:

Who	Paulsen's Challenge	How Paulsen Changed
Paulsen	to try to survive a bear attack; an emotional and physical challenge	He recognizes his insignificance to all of nature. Paulsen is somehow weakened by the experience.

Who	Character's Challenge	How Character Changed
Carl	World War II, physically and emotionally	He became an insecure, unstable, broken man.

I n d e x

Teacher's Guide page numbers are in parentheses following pupil's edition page numbers.

L e s s o n   T i t l e   I n d e x

Literature Index